Redefining the Three Rs

RELAX, REFOCUS, RECHARGE

by Anthony D. Fredericks

Rigby Best Teachers Press
An imprint of Rigby

Dedication

To Dawn Labadie
May her classroom be forever filled with life,
love, and laughter!

For more information about other books from Rigby Best Teachers Press,
please contact Rigby at 1-800-822-8661 or visit **www.rigby.com**.

Editors: Carol Allison
Executive Editor: Georgine Cooper
Designer: Biner Design
Design Project Manager: Tom Sjoerdsma
Cover artist: Margaret Cusack

08 07 06 05 04 03
9 8 7 6 5 4 3 2 1

ISBN 0-7398-7598-1
Reinventing the Three Rs: Relax, Refocus, Recharge

Library of Congress Cataloging-in-Publication Data

Fredericks, Anthony D.
  Redefining the three R's : relax, refocus, recharge / by Anthony D.
Fredericks.
     p. cm.
  ISBN 0-7398-7598-1
  1. Teachers--Psychology. 2. Teaching--Psychological aspects.
3. Stress management. I. Title: Redefining the 3 R's. II. Title.
  LB2840 .F72 2003
  371.1'01'9--dc21
                                        2002014535

Contents

Personal Growth

ATTITUDE

STRESS REDUCERS

SELF-IMPROVEMENT

A PLAN FOR PERSONAL GROWTH / 60

Relationship Growth

A NEW OUTLOOK

REACHING OUT

Professional Growth

Introduction

Many years ago, a graduate class instructor asked our class to participate in an activity that I will always remember. He asked each of us to bring in one 3" x 5" index card with our names on the front in large letters. Next we ruled the back of our cards into 60 1/2" x 1/2" squares. He asked us to carry the cards with us everywhere throughout the upcoming week.

The instructor then gave us an unusual set of instructions. He said that for each time someone said something negative to us, we were to tear out one of the squares on the card and discard it. If someone gave us a task to do that we did not choose to do, we were to tear out a square. If someone did not return our smile in the supermarket or hardware store, we were to tear out a square. If someone said an unkind word or failed to give us a compliment, we were to tear out a square. We were instructed to bring what was left of the cards to class the following week.

During the next week's class we all sat in a circle of chairs and shared our experiences with the cards. Most of us had a card that was significantly smaller than when we started. All had torn many pieces out of their cards. Our instructor informed us that the cards represented the amount of control each of us had over the slights and injustices of our daily lives. In other words, each tear-off was a way of letting go of the problems or negative situations we faced every day.

Our instructor made the point that each of us has control over the shape of our lives. If someone does something we do not like or says something inappropriate, we have the power to excise or discard that negative event from our lives.

Sometimes we may need to remove a large number of negative factors; at other times we may need to remove only a few. The point is that we have control over our individual cards in life. We are all dealt a different set of cards, but it is what each of us does with our respective cards that makes the difference. The most significant factor is that we can allow ourselves an unlimited supply of cards and unlimited license to discard petty problems and slights. The control is ours. We can hang on to the disruptions or frustrations of our daily lives, or we can take charge and remove them.

With so many demands on our time and so many tasks to be accomplished, it seems as though we teachers add more and more to our cards every day. As we dash around solving other people's problems or tackling the myriad of responsibilities imposed on us, we are pulled in so many directions at once that there is little of us left. We may have accomplished every task or solved every problem, but at what personal price?

In many ways, teachers' actions are often reactionary. That is, we react to a new set of curriculum standards, we react to a directive imposed by administration, we react to a phone call from an irate parent, or we react to the lack of adequate materials for an upcoming lesson. In a way, we develop a crisis mentality simply because we spend so much time responding to the needs, wishes, and wants of others.

Happily, there is another way to teach, a wholesome, enjoyable way that significantly reduces stress, makes us more productive as classroom teachers and human beings, and has a positive impact on our students. This alternative involves a change in attitude or perspective. It helps us refocus our priorities and reexamine the reasons we decided to become teachers in the first place.

This collection of strategies has been gathered from fellow teachers around the country—strategies that have been proven and validated by educators in almost every kind of school and locality. These ideas will help reduce your levels of stress and help you approach each day with a refreshed mind and a more relaxed perspective.

This book is written for teachers by a teacher, someone who, like you, has been in the trenches. Like you, I have dealt with both positive and negative experiences with school boards, administrators, colleagues, and students. Like you, I have crafted lesson plans, chased fugitive classroom hamsters, patched bruised knees and bruised egos, and dealt with concerned parents. In many ways, this is a true teacher's treasury, compiled from years of experience, scores of colleagues, and hundreds of students.

There are several ways to read this book. I would like to suggest that you not read it in one sitting. Dip in and out of the text; read two to three essays a day, think about them, and try to put them into action. Select one of the three major sections and select one or two chapters that you can identify with. Share the book with a group of friends. Select a single chapter, and plan some time when you can discuss the impact of its message. Read an essay from the back, read one from the middle, read another from the front. Take several weeks to slowly read and digest the suggestions offered. Pick and choose a few essays, and savor and reflect on their application to your life. There are many ways to enjoy this book.

Most importantly, this book will allow you to stand back and view the larger picture. You will discover powerful ideas that will help you refocus and relax. You will learn strategies that will reinvigorate your teaching as much as they will reinvigorate your life. You will read about techniques that help bring out more of the best in yourself. You will find ways to reduce the stress and the stressors in your teaching. I do not guarantee that all your problems will disappear. What I can offer you is renewed perspective and reinvigorated attitude. If you make these ideas part of your personal or professional curriculum, I am sure that you will discover a new energy and a renewed enjoyment of teaching.

Let's begin the journey!

Tony Fredericks

Acknowledgments

Throughout my teaching career I have been touched and influenced by many individuals. Former students, current colleagues, and friends far too numerous to mention have all shaped the views shared in this book. They are a beautiful part of my past and my present and I sincerely hope they will influence your present and future. For their unselfish assistance with this book, I celebrate the following:

To Gizz Davis, who brightens any classroom with his remarkable joie de vivre and insatiable appetite for life and learning, I extend my warmest and sincerest appreciation. Gizz is one of those rare individuals who influences those around him, not only with words, but by deeds and actions. It is truly an honor to call him both friend and colleague.

To Vicky Lynott, a friend who was there at the beginning and has always been a confidant, colleague, and integral part of my life, I extend a sincere and standing ovation. Vicky brings warmth and joy to all fortunate enough to have her as a friend. That she is also a teacher who touches students in magical and unforgettable ways is a testament to her philosophy and outlook on life.

To Stef Crumbling, who is one of the most engaging and positive teachers it has ever been my pleasure to know. As a former student, she brought life and laughter to every class. Now, as an educator, she shares the excitement of learning and the grins, giggles, and guffaws that should be part of every child's learning experiences. She is the crème de la crème of teachers.

For Cathy Swanson, who epitomizes the best in teachers today, I am truly and constantly amazed at the range of her creativity and the sincerity of her classroom projects and ventures. Countless students have benefited from her remarkable ideas and incredible spirit. So, too, have her love and laughter touched scores of friends and colleagues. She is a believer of the possible, an artisan of life, and a teacher of unparalleled imagination.

Tony Fredericks

Personal Growth

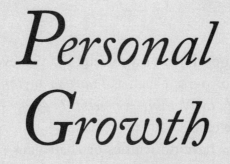

~ 1 ~

Accept Your Imperfections

Do you ever get down on yourself? Do you ever find yourself saying things to yourself such as *I can't do anything right, I'm just not good enough,* or *Nothing ever seems to go my way?* If you do, welcome to the club.

All of us have difficulties or challenges in our lives. We are able to tackle some successfully; others not as well. Very few of us can say that we are 100 percent successful in everything we do. It's just something we learn to accept as we mature and deal with some of the injustices and demands of the world.

Another truth we learn about our lives is that we are not perfect; we each have little imperfections in our personality or lack skill in a particular task that we must regularly face. However, the difference between individuals is often in how willing we are to accept our own personal imperfections. Psychologists tell us that an inability to embrace imperfection has a depressive influence on one's outlook and personality. In short, the negative conversations we have with ourselves are often due to our inability to accept the fact that we are not perfect.

Here is an example: I am known among family and friends as one of the world's worst singers. I cannot carry a tune, I sing off-key, and I can make even the most heartfelt love song sound like the screeching of truck tires on wet concrete. I tried out for choir three times in high school and was rejected each time. The simple fact is that I have never been, nor will I ever be, able to carry a tune. Nevertheless, I love to sing.

So, I sing. I hum in the shower, I whistle a tune when I walk down a hallway at work, and I sing out loud in the car as I drive across town. I accept that I am terrible at singing, but I do it anyway.

Whether it is due to heredity, nature, or environment, my lack of talent does not interfere with my joy in singing. I realize that I have a minor imperfection, and that is okay. Sure, I can bemoan the fact that I will never become a professional singer, but it will do me no good. I have come to accept it and move on.

Dwelling on imperfections can consume valuable time and energy. In the long run, it is counterproductive to a life of self-acceptance and happiness. Recognize that there are skills or talents you may never have and accept that. Focusing on those qualities that you *can* change will have a powerful effect on your attitude and self-acceptance.

For Reflection

❧ To be human is to be imperfect.

❧ Fool everyone—celebrate imperfections.

❧ Give up negative self-talk and watch imperfections decrease in importance.

❧ Turn an imperfection into a goal. How can you accept it or improve upon it?

~2~
What Is Truly Important

What is the most important thing you have done in your life? If you were to ask that question of many people, you might get responses such as *I worked my way through college and earned my degree,* or *I have been a teacher for x number of years and have influenced many lives,* or *I was able to start my own business and have been very successful.*

Most people, when asked, would single out an external event. They would identify a circumstance or situation that can be recognized by other people—a career, an award, an accomplishment, and an endeavor. How many people would identify self-improvement as the most important accomplishment? How many people would state one of the following?

I have learned to be more patient with other people.
I have learned how to live with my imperfections.
I have been able to reduce the stress in my life.
I now take time for myself each day.
I have discovered an inner peace I never had before.

When you think about it, we often identify accomplishments in terms of how they are perceived by other people. Our friends and family can see the new business we started. They can see the certificate that hangs on the wall. They can see the new house we purchased in a nice neighborhood. Are our greatest accomplishments those that can be *seen* by others or those *appreciated* by ourselves alone?

Take a few moments to look inside yourself. What do you see? More importantly, what do you see that has been created as the result of a conscious change in your outlook, demeanor, or attitude? What would you identify as your greatest internal accomplishment? Write it down.

You may discover, as I did, that this simple activity reaps tremendous rewards. It gives you the opportunity to celebrate the truly significant aspects of your life—your growth and development as a human being. It is also a signal that one accomplishment can trigger other equally important accomplishments. There is no end to the possibilities. Think about what is really important in your life. Is it what you have accomplished in the past, or is it what you are doing for yourself now?

For Reflection

❧ Do you know what your greatest internal accomplishment is?

❧ What do you see when you look inside yourself?

❧ Are you changing or are you standing still?

❧ If you could change one aspect about your life right now, what would it be and why are you waiting?

~3~

Congratulate Yourself

Recognizing your contributions from within yourself is . . .
more powerful and satisfying [than] hearing it from others.
Richard Carlson,
Don't Sweat the Small Stuff . . . and It's All Small Stuff

I once worked for an individual who never offered words of praise for employees' efforts or contributions to the school or district. When asked about this during a meeting, he replied, *You get all the appreciation you need in your pay envelope every other week!*

Unfortunately, there are people in the world who believe that pay is comparable to appreciation. They may not realize that pay is not appreciation, but rather compensation for services rendered. Few of us entered the field of teaching expecting high pay. We did not choose the teaching profession because of the six-figure salaries; we became teachers in spite of the five-figure salaries. Most of us entered the profession because we wanted to share our learning, to make a difference in the lives of children, and for the opportunities to positively influence their intellectual, social, and emotional growth.

Every so often, it is important for us to stop and give ourselves a much-needed pat on the back. We need to think about the growth we have stimulated in our students, how our students have matured intellectually, and how we have influenced their lives. It is valuable for us to mentally review our accomplishments, and once in a while, we need to reward ourselves.

It is easy to get caught up in lesson plans, scheduling, evaluating new materials, or letters to parents. But it is even more important to regularly take time to celebrate us. We need to review our accomplishments and honor ourselves for the work we are doing. Because we are often the best evaluators of our work, it is important that we regularly acknowledge and praise our own efforts.

Richard Carlson, the author of *Don't Sweat the Small Stuff . . . and It's All Small Stuff,* says that, "Praise from others is never a certainty, and making it a condition of your happiness is really a bad idea." What he means is that although we all need praise and encouragement on a regular basis we should not base our actions on the expectation of that praise.

My own strategy is to schedule a time at the end of each week for self-assessment and self-reward. I find a quiet place and time to mentally review the week and focus on some of its accomplishments. This procedure takes about five minutes, but it makes such a big difference. Celebrate yourself, reaffirm the good things you do, and recognize your role in the lives of young people. A self-administered reward is the best kind of appreciation of all!

For Reflection

❧ When was the last time you rewarded yourself?

❧ Reach around and give yourself a good pat on the back.

❧ Take time, regularly, to celebrate what you do and how you do it.

❧ Above all, be good to yourself.

~4~
Who You Truly Are

Select five friends and ask them this question: *If you could be anyone in the world, who would you be?* How did they answer? Did they give the name of a famous movie star, a national political figure, a wealthy businessperson, or a world-renowned author? Did any of them submit his or her name?

If you could be anybody, who would you be? This may sound like a popular parlor game or teenage discussion question, but what makes it even more interesting is how many people would choose to be someone else. Because someone in the world possesses something they do not, such as money, power, fame, or beauty, they might want to be that person.

I suppose that in this age of assessment, we are inclined to compare people with one another. We certainly do a great deal of that in education. Each student is tested, assessed, and evaluated in terms of how she or he compares with other students. They are graded or evaluated according to a set of standards created by someone else. Seldom do we evaluate students in comparison with themselves and their abilities.

What makes this all the more interesting is that we often do the same thing to ourselves. We wish we could be our colleague down the hall in her ability to teach math. We wish we could be our teammate who can design the world's greatest science lesson. We wish we could be our coworker who always has the neatest classroom and the most organized schedule in the entire school. Wishing that we could be someone we are not means our time and thoughts are occupied in nonproductive ways.

Wishing takes time away from working on the person we can become. Certainly, we can admire the behaviors and attitudes of others. It is when we seek to *become* those individuals that we exhaust the power of our own possibilities. This behavior becomes self-defeating as we lose the inner perspective and personal focus necessary to self-improvement.

Like you, I admire the talents and accomplishments of others whose attributes become models for me. I may ask myself the question, *How can I become more organized?* instead of *I wish I were Jonas; he's so organized.* The first statement is a personal goal; the second is a wish. The first gives me something to aim for and requires energy to achieve change; the second consumes my time and saps my energy for no change.

Is there something you appreciate in another person? That's okay; use that quality as a model for self-improvement, a focal point for self-initiated growth.

For Reflection

❧ Appreciate those you admire. Use them as models for your own growth.

❧ Become yourself, not someone else's expectation of who you should be.

❧ Loving yourself is not a selfish act.

❧ Remember the armed forces' recruiting slogan, *Be all you can be!*

~5~
Be Grateful

I touch the future, I teach.
Christa McAuliffe

Wouldn't it be great if we all made a six-figure salary, had complete control over the curriculum, felt always appreciated, and enjoyed a teacher's lounge staffed with a personal masseuse?

As the popular song title says, "You Can't Always Get What You Want." The reality is that life is not perfect, and we seldom get everything we wish for. Some may argue that life is not fair, and they are right. Life is not fair. Life is full of bumps, twists, and turns, potholes and dead ends, and other challenges along the road. Life is not about being fair. It's about what we do with the cards we are dealt.

It is quite easy to complain about what we do not have, and we all do it to some extent. How we celebrate what we do have is most important. How often do we celebrate the fact that we do have a job? How often do we celebrate the fact that we play a role in shaping the lives of others? How often do we celebrate the fact that we have a roof over our heads, enough to eat, and a warm bed to sleep in at night? How often do we celebrate the fact that we have an education that provides us with incredible learning opportunities? How often do we stop to celebrate the life we have, instead of bemoaning the things we do not?

Yes, we all want to improve our lives. We all want better lives, but it's counterproductive to concentrate on the things we lack instead of appreciating what we have. Complaining is easy; celebrating requires a little more effort.

A simple strategy I use is to wake up each morning and make a conscious decision to celebrate something I am grateful for, such as my family, my friends, my job, and my health. That celebration becomes part of my daily activities. I may take a few moments to compose a brief note to myself at lunch, steal a few minutes to compose a mental image at the end of the day, or say a silent thank you before retiring at night. Whatever the celebration, it is important to count my blessings. Celebrations don't have to be long, but they are important in helping me recognize what is truly important in my life. This strategy may take a little bit of effort, but I think you will find interesting revelations about the present and will gain a fresh perspective on the future.

For Reflection

❧ Know what is really important in your life. Celebrate it!

❧ Be sure to know the difference between the things you want in life and the things you need.

❧ As the old saying goes, "The best things in life are free."

❧ Be grateful for what you have.

~ 6 ~
What Do You Like About Yourself?

I learned this technique from a friend several years ago. She helped me realize that who we are as individuals is determined not so much by the thoughts or comments of others, but, most importantly, by the thoughts and comments we have about ourselves.

Sharon maintains a personal daily diary. In it she writes her thoughts, ruminations, and feelings about her life and the career she has chosen. On Monday mornings though, she does something different. She gets up a half-hour earlier each Monday morning and uses that time to write something special in her diary. She always begins it the same way: "Five things I like about myself."

Sharon has discovered that this small bit of time reflecting on the things she enjoys most about herself is her buffer against the world around her. She says that by taking the time to ponder and reinforce the goodness within herself, she can face the week with renewed energy and a reinvigorated self-concept.

We all go through times when things do not go our way. The clerk at the department store may not treat us as kindly as we would like. The person who returns our dry cleaning may not be in a good mood. Someone may cut us off in traffic. A supervisor may not return a message or provide a service we asked for. We often take these events personally. We sometimes take offense and our mood changes accordingly.

Too often, we carry around bad feelings about a negative event or encounter. We may even internalize those events and say to ourselves, *Gee, that person doesn't like me* or *I must have done something wrong, maybe it was my fault*. The actions of others may shape how we think about ourselves. Often, those beliefs tend to wear us down because we carry them around for extended periods of time.

To deflect those thoughts, I'd like to suggest that you, like my friend Sharon, take a few moments at the start of each week to record five things that you like about yourself. You may wish to write these on an index card and place it in the top drawer of your desk. Every once in a while throughout the week open the drawer and peek in. Use that brief moment to remind yourself of the things that make you special—the strengths you recognize in yourself.

I think we spend too much time thinking about or worrying about what others think about us, what they say about us, or how they react to us. By taking some time to celebrate the things that you *know* to be true about yourself, you obtain approval from the most important person in our life—you! What we think about ourselves and how we celebrate that knowledge can be a powerful motivating force.

For Reflection

⚜ Regularly, take time to note what you like about you.

⚜ Worry less about the opinions of others and more about what you think about you.

⚜ Remind yourself that your frame of mind will ultimately determine the mood of your day.

⚜ Do you like you?

~ 7 ~
Recognize the Magic Inside

Have you even seen the movie *Dumbo,* the animated story of a young elephant who wants to fly but is afraid to do so? His friend, a mouse, gives him a feather and tells him that the feather is a magic one, needed in order to fly. Dumbo grasps the feather in his trunk and discovers that he can fly. One day, while perched near the top of a circus tent, Dumbo loses the feather. The only way down is by flying. His mouse friend urges him on and eventually Dumbo takes flight. What he discovers is that the feather wasn't magic, rather, the magic was inside him.

How many of us turn to books and magazines in search of the perfect recipe of life or the secret formula that will make us eternally happy or perpetually rich? How many of us depend on self-help books, tapes, videos, and other popular methods to provide us with inspiration and direction in our lives? We keep searching and searching for the magic elixir for happiness.

I am not suggesting that we give up our search for happiness. Nor am I suggesting that the books and tapes we purchase are not worthwhile. I am suggesting, however, that most guidelines and admonitions are based on a simple truth— the magic of our lives lies within us. Purchasing a book will not make us happy. Listening to a pop psychologist extol the virtues of a simple life will not bring joy. Watching a TV program on a new psychological movement will not guarantee great riches or eternal satisfaction.

The ultimate factor for change in our lives lies within our hearts and minds. One of the most powerful things I learned some time ago was to be grateful for who I am and to recognize the power within. Like you, I want to improve my life. I want to grow, develop, and become a better human being. That growth process does not come about because of any external force or element, a magic feather, for example. It comes from within ourselves.

The suggestion is simple. Look for the internal magic and take advantage of it. When you wake up in the morning, take a few moments to recognize and celebrate the magical powers you already have. You will find yourself involved in a day of incredible possibilities and zestful experiences.

For Reflection

❧ Look for the magic inside you.

❧ The answers to your life's mysteries might be close to your heart or near to your mind.

❧ Self-help does not always come from a book; it comes from within.

~8~

Be Nice to Yourself

Growing up, I was always admonished, *If you can't say something nice about someone, don't say anything at all.* There is a lot of truth in that axiom. We should be kind and pleasant to the people around us. We should celebrate others in a positive way.

I think it important to be nice to other people, but I also think it is important to be kind to oneself. We are usually pleasant to those around us, but we often fail to take time to be good to ourselves. The following exercise will help you do just that in a systematic way.

First, choose someone you encountered today and think of something kind to say about that person. If you are like most people, you will think of something that is subjective, such as *She had a nice hairstyle, I really liked the tie he wore,* or *She did a good job with the class play.*

The next step is to think of something honest about that individual. When you think of something honest, you will tend to think of something that is very factual in nature, such as *She got her new hairdo at Michael's Hair Salon, He wore a red and yellow tie today,* or *Her class put on a 30-minute play.*

Now think of something that is both honest and nice to say. Focus on a very specific aspect of the individual, and add your own personal comments or reflections on a specific quality. For example, *The new hairdo she got at Michael's really complements her face, His bold and brash tie really made him stand out in the school photograph,* or *Her class play gave every child a chance to shine.*

What does this sequence of pleasantries have to do with you? Plenty. Kindness and honesty about others create positive thought processes that enable you to treat yourself to genuine kindness.

Identify a specific time of day when you have a few moments to yourself. This may be as soon as you get up in the morning, while you are in the shower, or on your way to school. During this time, think of something honestly pleasant about yourself. Please remember our rules above and be as specific as you can. For example, *I really helped Carolyn get the materials together for the History Day project, I did a good job in designing the class garden yesterday,* or *I really look pretty sharp with my new hairstyle today.* The important thing is that the comment be both *pleasant* and *honest.*

Take an additional few moments to write down your thoughts. You may wish to purchase an inexpensive diary and make it a habit to write down something honest and kind about yourself every day. Your comment can be about an event or circumstance from the previous day, or it can be a reflection on your day. Occasionally, take time to review your comments. Reward yourself with generous amounts of kindness.

For Reflection

❧ Plan regular times to honor yourself.

❧ What you say about yourself and what you believe to be true about yourself may be the most important observations of the day.

❧ Let yourself know who is important in your life.

❧ Record the nice things you know to be true about you. Review them on a regular basis.

~9~

Count All Your Riches

Driving home from work the other day, I began to notice the little bulletins posted on telephone poles. I am not sure what drew my attention to these simple notices that had been tacked up to various poles in and around town. A great number of them proclaimed *Get rich in just 90 days while you work at home*, or *Want to make a lot of money without a lot of work? Just call 555–1212*, or *Never have to work again—own your own business.* The object of these notices is to entice people to call a certain phone number, turn over a sum of money to a stranger, and receive the key to lifelong riches.

Many of these are scams designed to do nothing more than take innocent victims' money and leave them with empty promises. They also take advantage of a human desire for large sums of money with little output of time or energy. *Make lots of money,* they entice, *and you will be eternally happy!*

We tend to look to external sources for happiness and joy while some of our greatest assets might be right in front of us. It is often a great revelation to discover that the simplest things in our lives are the greatest riches. The first time our child says *mama* or *dada*, a greeting card sent by a long lost friend, the sunrise over a mountaintop while on vacation, a surprise from a spouse, a compliment from a total stranger—these are the true riches of life. Too often, we take simple things for granted. The result is an *expectation*, rather than an *appreciation*.

We can learn to focus on the simple things in our lives and celebrate what is near to us, rather than merely aspire to those out of reach. Strive to begin each day with an appreciation of one element, one person, or one event already in your life. Honor what is close at hand, and you will feel refreshed and revitalized.

For Reflection

❧ Your happiness may be right in front of you.

❧ Celebrate your life as it is today.

❧ Know that we create our own riches—riches unrelated to money.

❧ Appreciate the simple, honor the near, and embrace the beauty.

~10~

What Really Makes You Happy

What gives you joy? Is it the cooing of your newborn child, the glow of a bright moon on a summer night, an affectionate touch, the greeting of the family dog when you get home from work, or a moment of silent contemplation following a rewarding day? Perhaps, the question we might ask ourselves is *What makes me, as an individual, truly happy?*

Often, particularly in our work, we spend a large part of our lives trying to make other people happy. We work hard to ensure the happiness of our students. We complete a report or turn in a lesson plan on time to keep our supervisor happy. We visit a sick friend or send a greeting card for someone's birthday so that they might be happy. We make a phone call knowing that the other person will be happy with some recent news or announcement.

As loving, caring individuals we are deeply committed to the happiness of others. As teachers, we feel a special responsibility to ensure that joy and happiness are part of the lives of others. That is simply the nature of most individuals in our profession. One of the reasons we decided to become teachers was to impart the joy of learning to others.

As teachers, we are often selfless and giving. That does not mean, however, that we should neglect our own happiness. It is important to take time each day to recognize and celebrate the things that bring us joy and happiness. You may be surprised to discover the internal satisfaction that can occur when you take a few moments each day to think about something that makes you truly happy.

Not too long ago I was under pressure of a very tight deadline to edit a children's book manuscript. It meant very long days in front of my computer, writing and revising. Things were going slowly, and I was not sure I would be able to complete all the corrections my editor had suggested. As the deadline approached, I was getting more and more anxious and was spending more and more time in my office. One morning my wife walked in the office, embraced me, gave me a kiss, and told me how much she loved me. After she left, I realized how truly happy she had made me.

When I returned to my manuscript, I realized that I had been so involved with my work that I had not taken the time to focus on what was important. The manuscript was completed on time and seemed to have more zip. Even more important was the realization that the sources of happiness may be right in front of us. We only need to take the time to recognize, savor, and embrace them.

For Reflection

❧ Happiness will find you if your heart is ready.

❧ Don't ignore the possibilities for happiness. They may be close at hand.

❧ What truly makes you happy? Is it close at hand?

❧ Do you look for happiness or does happiness find you?

~11~
Take Some Time to Walk

There is a part of the day that I look forward to with great expectation and anticipation. It is when I am able to step outside the door to my house with the dog on the leash and walk down the roads, up the hills, and through the woods surrounding our neighborhood. I may discover a newly constructed bird's nest, a fallen tree, a smooth and polished rock by the road, or some new tracks in the mud. My dog undoubtedly will discover new items to sniff, new paths to explore, and new sounds that perk her ears. This is a time of discovery for both of us—discovery of things both simple and new.

These are also times when I can escape the responsibilities that await me, the endless succession of phone calls and email messages, and the parade of tasks on the endless *To Do* list. On two different levels, these daily walks are critical to my inner fulfillment.

In a sense, I see myself as an explorer, one who seeks what is over the horizon or just beyond the next hill. I like to seek out the unknown—never sure of what I'm going to find but sure that there might be a new adventure waiting for me. The anticipation of what might be, as opposed to the daily knowledge of what is, is both creative and dynamic. The discoveries need not be grand; they need only be newly discovered.

In another sense, these ramblings through our semi-rural area provide me with mental refreshment. It is an opportunity to become inwardly focused, to assess my present being, and to take stock of how I have grown. This is an opportunity for me to achieve a deeper awareness of who I am and where I'm going. Undisturbed by life's demands, I can reflect on personal serenity.

Unlike some more rigorous programs of exercise or fitness, daily walks are opportunities to discover and learn. Whether you live in the middle of a large city or rural environment, there is much to discover in the world around you. You are not in search of grand discoveries, but for opportunities to observe the little things that would go unnoticed if you were speeding by in a car. Use this time for self-reflection and self-renewal. Look into yourself and evaluate what you see. How have you changed? Have you improved? Have you grown? Are you in the process of *becoming* or are you *complete*?

Daily walks are as much for the mind and soul as for the body. By taking time for yourself, you will discover unique and unplanned opportunities for exploration—exploration of the little things in your environment and, more importantly, discovery of the things that are important to your growth and development as a human being.

For Reflection

❧ Plan some time to explore your immediate world—you may make some amazing discoveries.

❧ Walking without interruption can bring peace and harmony into a hectic day.

❧ Think of walking as a tonic for the soul and refreshment for the mind.

❧ Put on your shoes, open the door, and go!

~I2~

Is There Enough Play in Your Life?

A few years ago I wrote a monthly column for an education magazine. The column, entitled *Parent Talk* provided classroom teachers with tips, advice, and suggestions on how they could encourage and maintain more parent involvement in classroom activities. One month, after reading several articles about how rushed and hectic family lives have become, I decided to write an article on play.

Through research, I have discovered that play is something that is missing from the lives of many families. Parents are working longer hours, kids are involved in an enormous variety of after-school activities, and weekends are consumed by demands of the family *To Do* list. It seems as though family members have forgotten to include sufficient playtime in their daily interactions with each other.

I suspect that we, too, fail to plan enough playtime in our lives. We become so focused on the needs of our students or the demands of our administrators that we do not allow for some *time out* in our daily lives—time to play, no goals, no behavioral objectives, and no deadlines.

We often think of playtime as nonproductive time. Nothing is produced, nothing is learned, nothing is accomplished, so why should we include it in our busy daily lives? We think playtime is for kids, not adults. Psychologists tell us that children need sufficient playtime opportunities in order to achieve balance and perspective in their lives. If that is true for children, why not also true for adults?

When was the last time you played? Was it last week? Was it last month?, or was it so long ago that you cannot remember? I am not suggesting that play is something that should be scheduled into your daily activities. Rather, it should be spontaneous and free. It can be as simple as pulling out a crossword puzzle during a meeting. It can be swinging on a swing at the local playground, flying a kite in your backyard, or assembling a jigsaw puzzle instead of watching TV.

Not too long ago I was flying home from Orlando where I had been a visiting children's author. It was a Friday night, and the airplane was packed with businesspeople returning home after a week of meetings, appointments, and consultations. Every seat was filled, and each person had a laptop computer, spreadsheet, or business document on a tray table. Every person was intently focused on work. About two seats in front of me, a young girl sat in the aisle seat. On her table were a coloring book and a small box of crayons. She was casually coloring in the outlines of several theme park characters. I noticed that she was the only one whistling and the only one on the entire plane who was smiling.

Get a box of crayons. Play.

For Reflection

♣♭ When was the last time you played?

♣♭ Make play a regular part of your day. Trust me, something interesting will happen.

♣♭ Reread the last two sentences of this essay. Go ahead and do it.

~13~
Resist the Urge to Compare

Since you are like no other being ever created since
the beginning of time, you are incomparable.
Brenda Ueland

When you were growing up did you ever hear relatives say things like, *Oh, you're so much like your Aunt Edna,* or *You have your mother's eyes and your father's nose,* or *You remind me of your cousin Will—you know, the one who became a doctor.* Like you, I was compared to every relative ever recorded on the pages of the family Bible and probably a few who were not.

We are, by nature, an evaluative society. One of the longest-running buzz phrases in American education is the term *authentic assessment.* We use that term to refer to the multitude of assessment procedures that provide a true picture of a student's progress through a subject or grade level.

The evaluation process has a down side. In short, we are often compared to others. We are measured *by* our peers, and we are measured *against* our peers. Who we are is often determined by measuring up to our relatives, friends, or colleagues. We are made to feel more of a comparative object than an individual person.

Rather than allow yourself to be measured by others, measure yourself. Your self-evaluation is intrinsically more important and certainly more meaningful than any other assessment. After all, who knows you better than you do?

If someone says to you, *You remind me of so and so,* don't allow him or her to complete the sentence. Encourage them to tell you exactly what you do or how you behave without inserting a comparative example. By the same token, don't fall into the habit of comparing others. Judge each individual on personal merits and avoid bringing another individual into the picture.

Here is the most important point: Avoid comparing *yourself* to others. Admire the qualities of other human beings but avoid measuring yourself against their standards. It is what we see in ourselves that is most important. The key to achieving harmony in our lives is to look inward. It may be a revealing examination, and it most certainly is a way of achieving peace and harmony.

For Reflection

🌿 Who you want to become is more important than who you want to be like.

🌿 Judge yourself against your own standards, not against standards created by others.

🌿 Your growth is more important than someone else's attainment.

~14~

Make Stretching Part of Your Daily Routine

Do you feel stressed out by the end of the day? Are you uptight? Are you tense and irritable? If you are like many teachers, you experience an emotional and physical low by the end of the day. You cannot wait to get home and R-E-L-A-X.

Teachers spend much of their day in high gear. We handle one "emergency" after another, manage one teaching unit after another, and fulfill others' needs on demand throughout the day. Our daily schedule is a nonstop express from beginning to end.

In our hustle and bustle lives we sometimes forget that we need to fuel our emotional, cognitive, and physical components. We spend so much time tending to the cognitive skills that we often neglect the other parts of our *machine*.

One way to recharge and re-energize is by taking five or ten minutes in the middle of the day to engage in simple stretching exercises. A number of books available on the market contain simple exercises that can be done with a minimum of time or effort in the comfort of your classroom. I have found that isometric exercises work best for me. They are easy to do and can be incorporated into my daily routine. Here are a few to get you started:

A Leg Up: Sit in your chair with your back straight and your feet firmly on the floor. Slowly lift both legs until your body forms an L shape. Hold that position for a count of ten. Lower your feet to the floor. Repeat ten times.

Neck Stretch: Reach up with your right hand and place it on the left side of your head. Slowly pull your head down to your right shoulder. Straighten your head and repeat ten times. Repeat the procedure with your left hand and pull your head down to your left shoulder. Repeat ten times.

Chest Stretch: Stand up straight. Bring your arms straight behind you and clasp your hands together behind your back. Raise your shoulders slowly up and then slowly down. Repeat ten times.

Twist and Shout: Stand up straight. Touch your right shoulder with your right hand and your left shoulder with your left hand. Slowly turn your upper torso to the left. Return to the starting position and slowly turn your upper torso to the right. Keep your feet in the same place each time. Repeat ten times.

Push Off: Stand approximately two feet away from a wall. Fall toward the wall with your hands firmly on the surface. Do a simulated push-up from the wall by letting your head come close to the wall and then pushing off with your hands. Repeat this ten times.

Isometric exercises can be done quickly at any time of the day. You will discover that regular exercise is an ideal way to keep your body flexible and allow you time to focus on matters unrelated to your job. The result is less stress.

For Reflection

❧ Plan stretch time as part of your daily routine.

❧ Remember that stress reduction involves both body and soul.

❧ Move your body, and you will be better prepared to move your mind.

~15~

Don't Allow Other People's Problems to Become Yours

As I was driving in to work the other day on a road slick from an overnight ice storm, I needed to navigate cautiously the hills and blind curves. As I was driving along at a safe speed for the conditions, a pair of headlights rapidly approached me from the rear. In a few moments the driver was *directly* behind me with not more than a few inches separating our bumpers. It was obvious that the driver was in a hurry and thought that if he tailgated me, he would be able to increase my speed and get to his destination faster.

The rural road provided no opportunities for the car to pass nor for me to pull over. I became increasingly nervous about his dangerous driving. I worried that an animal might run in front of my car, or I might slide on an icy curve, and the tailgater would plow into my car.

As I became more anxious about the situation, it occurred to me that I was allowing his inconsiderate behavior to become my concern. His tardiness to work or his inability to maintain a safe speed on a slick road was now becoming my problem.

I began to realize that other people have the potential to increase our stress in many ways. Their attempt to control us by exerting pressure on us enables them to alleviate their immediate problem. In short, we become *their* victims at *our* own expense.

I am not suggesting that we become inconsiderate individuals. What I am suggesting is that we avoid assuming the responsibilities of people who would expect us to compensate for a deficit in their actions, character, or attitude. It is important that we understand that ultimately we are responsible for ourselves, not for the actions or lack of action of others.

We want to be helpful when a friend asks, *I've got a problem. Can you help me out?* That is because there is a mutual understanding and respect between two individuals. I enjoy helping friends and strangers in situations as simple as reaching for a cereal box on the top of a grocery shelf for an elderly shopper or as deep as comforting a colleague at the death of a parent. These situations of help and concern are invitational, not demanding.

Just because the driver behind me on the road has a problem, I do not need to be the one to provide the solution. My immediate concern is to maintain a safe driving speed and arrive at work safe and sound. The individual behind me needs to take responsibility for his poor planning; it is not my problem.

For Reflection

❧ Don't assume the negativity of others.

❧ Just because someone else is having a bad day, it doesn't have to become your bad day.

❧ Help others when invited, not necessarily when demanded.

❧ Be true to yourself.

~16~

Taking Care of You

Love the kids, love the job,
but take time to love yourself.
Stef Crumbling, fourth-grade teacher, York, PA

As teachers, we often find ourselves exhausted at the end of the day. We cannot wait for the weekend or the next vacation period. If we have a family, we discover that the added responsibilities of family life often make us grouchy, irritable, or just plain overworked. Thoughts of a new career seem tempting. Some of us are just trying to hang on until retirement; others are burning out.

Many of us chose teaching careers because we wanted to give something to others. We wanted to share our knowledge and expertise with a new generation of students. We wanted to stimulate the intellectual growth of youngsters with a variety of activities and a variety of learning experiences. We became teachers because we wanted to make a difference in other people's lives. Little did we know how exhausting and how tiring all of that would be!

After 20 or 30 years in the classroom, how are some teachers able to approach each day with the same vigor and energy they had when they first began teaching? How are they able to continue to create exciting lesson plans and dynamic units that inspire their students week after week and month after month? How are they able to achieve balance in their personal and professional lives?

These are all good questions, and they all engender the same response. The key to success as classroom teachers lies in our ability to take care of ourselves. Devote time and energy to your own well-being, self-renewal, and personal objectives. Caring for ourselves does not mean that we become self-centered or selfish. Caring for ourselves is a significant factor in the physical, emotional, and mental balance we need to maintain our stamina.

What it all boils down to is this: We cannot take care of others until we first take care of ourselves. Teachers who give so much to others that they have little left for themselves begin to burn out. They lose touch with the core of their existence and with the magic of self-renewal that is within all of us. When you commit yourself to becoming the best you can be you will discover a new energy, a new serenity, and a new spirit of giving that will empower you to help others. As you empower those around you, you will become a better teacher and a better human being!

For Reflection

❧ Taking care of yourself is not a selfish act—it is a necessary and personal one.

❧ If you are not whole, it will be difficult to assist others in becoming whole.

❧ Physical growth and emotional growth start from the inside out.

~17~
Create a Personal To Do List

Like most teachers I write regular *To Do* lists. I have lists for daily activities, weekly assignments, and long-range projects. Depending on the day or time of year, some lists are extensive; others are brief. Like you, I go through the lists, and as I complete each task, I place a check mark in front of each to note that it has been accomplished. When all items on the list have been checked off, I toss the list in the wastebasket and set about creating a new *To Do* list for the next round of tasks.

Not too long ago I was faced with an extensive *To Do* list. More than 20 items filled the front of a self-adhesive note. The tasks were written in blue ink, and those that had been completed were prefaced with a red check mark. I had assigned myself several short-term projects and many long-range projects. As I reviewed the list, it became clear that something was lacking. All of the tasks I had listed were for the benefit of others. I had not given myself any personal objectives.

Most teachers are naturally altruistic. Part of our nature and our life's work is based on giving to others. We are successful because we want the best for our students and for those with whom we work. We devote much of our time and energy to the improvement of others. We dedicate ourselves to helping others develop, learn, and grow in productive ways.

But unanswered questions remain: What is on the *To Do* list for us? What projects, activities, or assignments can we put on the list that will help us develop, learn, and grow? Does our list lack sufficient opportunities for taking care of our needs?

We need to provide and *schedule* regular and sustained time for ourselves each day. This may include time to read the next chapter in a favorite book, time to slip into a pair of running shoes and jog, time to find a quiet place to meditate, time to treat ourselves to a back rub or massage, or time to listen to soft music. What is important is that our daily *To Do* list allows us time for ourselves.

Without scheduled times for personal tasks, we can get all caught up in our responsibilities to others. We tend to neglect ourselves, and pretty soon we are drained, exhausted, and emotionally depleted. We are in a state of unbalance that fosters stress, tiredness, and anxiety.

The next time you create a *To Do* list, plan *to do* something for yourself. Make it a regular practice, and you will discover that other tasks can be tackled with increased levels of vigor and determination.

For Reflection

❧ What have you done for yourself lately?

❧ Are you doing so much for others that you are not doing enough for yourself?

❧ Do you regularly schedule time for yourself during the week?

❧ Where does all of your time go?

~18~

Think About What You Want in Life

Whatever the mind can conceive and believe . . .
it can achieve.
Napoleon Hill

What do you believe in? Do you believe every one of your students can achieve? Do you believe that you can become a better person? Do you believe that you can make as much difference in your own life as you make in the lives of others?

Are you a dreamer? More importantly, are you one who takes action on her or his dreams? Do you consciously work at making your dreams become reality? How are you making that happen?

Whatever we *believe* will happen often *does* happen. It is called a self-fulfilling prophecy. If we see nothing but success for each of our students, then we work to help that success become a reality. On the other hand, if we believe that our students have little potential, they tend to live up to our perception and achieve little success.

What do you believe about yourself? Do you see yourself as a successful teacher or a successful human being? If so, you probably engage in practices and procedures that help achieve teaching success. Or, do you see yourself stuck in a dead-end job with little chance for improvement or advancement? What is the result of that line of thinking? Ideas that you imagine or think about may come true.

The truth is that we need to prepare our minds to achieve happiness in life. The mental foundation we build serves as the launching pad for our dreams and aspirations. Self-improvement follows self-preparation. Knowing how we wish to grow depends on planting the seeds of growth in our own minds.

Think about your aspirations; dream and imagine. Remember to make a mental note to *believe* that they can happen. Visualize success. Convince yourself that your dreams are possible. *Believing* is often a critical first step in *making* things happen.

For Reflection

❧ Have you prepared yourself for what you truly want in life?

❧ Take time to make your dreams become reality.

❧ Believing you can succeed is the first step; the second step is up to you.

~19~

Take Action for Your Life

There comes a time in the affairs of men when we must
grab the bull by the tail and face the situation.
W. C. Fields

Are you a responsible person? You would probably answer *Yes*
to that question simply because most teachers attend to assigned
tasks and fulfill their duties. You do those tasks faithfully and
honestly, right?

Allow me to ask that question in another way. Do you
accept responsibility for yourself? You might be inclined to answer
in the affirmative simply because you live with yourself first, and
then you live with others. You take care of yourself physically and
mentally, and you feel pretty good about who you are and what you
are doing in life. Of course, you are responsible for yourself!

I would like to suggest another perspective on this question. The idea is a modification of one in Dr. Philip McGraw's
book *Life Strategies: Doing What Works, Doing What Matters*. Dr.
McGraw states that people need to spend more time resolving,
rather than enduring their personal problems. His focus is on
the fact that we often spend more time and effort resolving the
difficulties and challenges of other people when we should take
the time to address our own personal problems. I agree with his
thesis, but I also see another point of view.

We do not grow as loving and committed human beings unless we take charge of our own lives. You and I and a couple of billion other people in the world face challenges and difficulties every day. The difference is how we perceive those personal challenges. Are we willing to accept the shortcomings or deficiencies in our lives? Do we endure our imperfections and *dog paddle* our way through life? Are we content with our personal status quo?

Conversely, are we willing to take action, to put ourselves in charge of our self-development and self-improvement? The resolution of a problem is usually not evolutionary; it requires determination and action. It requires someone to take the initiative, to take charge, and to storm ahead. Time alone does not solve problems; they are solved because someone decides plans to take action and then acts.

I believe that the best person to solve my problems or improve my imperfections is myself. Certainly, I will take advice from friends and family, and I will read the advice of experts and counselors. Ultimately, I am the one who makes the decision or takes the action. I am responsible for me. Are you responsible for you?

For Reflection

❧ Are you willing to take action toward self-improvement?

❧ Are you content with the status quo, or are you willing to take risks now and then?

❧ Do you have the spunk to change the most significant individual in your life?

❧ Where are you going?

~20~

Your Definition of Success

To believe your own thought, to believe that what is true for you in your private heart is true for all men—that is genius.
Ralph Waldo Emerson

How do you define success? Place a check mark in front of each of the following statements that you sincerely believe to be true about yourself. Remember that this is a self-test, so be true to you!

____ I have limitations, and I accept them.
____ I take time each day for myself—no one else, just me.
____ I am grateful for the people in my life.
____ I love, I am in love, and I am loved.
____ I have made mistakes, but I have made peace with those mistakes.
____ There is peace and serenity in my life.
____ I take care of my needs.
____ There is passion in my life.
____ I regularly celebrate my achievements, both large and small.
____ I dream.
____ I believe that "A smile is a window to the soul."
____ I laugh at myself and with others.
____ I share the real *me* with other people.
____ I embrace change—in myself and in the world in which I live.
____ Children are my favorite teachers.

How did you do? Did you place a check mark in front of all or most of the statements above? Which ones did you have to think about? Which ones were you unsure of?

People often define success as something that is won. For example, a professional tennis player is successful if she wins several tournaments in her career. A businessman is successful if his company's stock improves. The person down the street is successful if he has won the lottery. We view success as a game or contest.

Real success is personal. Real success in life is understanding yourself, your values, and your qualities as a human being. True success is not accumulating lots of points, money, or fame; it is being in touch with you. Most importantly, it is acknowledging the value of your personal qualities and being grateful for what you have to share with others.

For Reflection

❧ Are you a successful person?

❧ Is your definition of success consistent with your personal goals in life?

❧ Remember that the best kind of success is that which we create for ourselves, not that achieved in a contest where the rules are determined by others.

❧ True success is never measured, but it can be attained.

~21~

Make an Appointment with Yourself

This unusual strategy can be a powerful way for us to take stock of who we are and where we are.

Make a daily appointment with yourself. That's right—when you plan your activities for the day or schedule appointments for the week, plan some time for *you* to meet with *you*. In the daily hustle and bustle of everyday duties and responsibilities, we get caught up in giving more and more of ourselves to others. There is certainly nothing wrong with that, but what frequently results is that there is little of ourselves left at the end of the day. We are tired, exhausted, and drained, both physically and emotionally.

You need time for yourself, and it needs to be scheduled. If you are like me, you keep an appointment calendar. You schedule an appointment with your dentist, a meeting with a colleague, a doctor's appointment, a birthday celebration, or a social engagement. By writing those dates on your appointment calendar, you are reminded to keep them.

I am suggesting that you schedule time for yourself. Each day, write down a time in your calendar to be spent on you. This may be a period of time in which you read a chapter of a favorite novel, listen to your favorite music, engage in some mental imagery, or simply look out the window and appreciate the view. It is your time—time set aside just for you. This appointment is no less important than an appointment with your doctor or an appointment to meet a friend for lunch.

Commit a part of your day to yourself, and you will find an opportunity to collect your thoughts, refresh your spirit, and reinvigorate yourself. Go ahead. Schedule time in your calendar right now. You will be glad you did. I guarantee it.

For Reflection

❧ Take some time for yourself.

❧ Don't let your spiritual or mental *fuel tank* get close to empty. Refill it on a regular basis.

❧ Doing more for yourself will help you do more for others

~22~

Establish Self-Rewarding Rituals

I began writing this book in December 2000. During that year, I had nine new books published—six were teacher books and three were children's books. It was a very good year. Overall, I've had the pleasure of writing more than 80 books.

The first time I meet people to talk about my writing, the question I am most asked is *How do you find the time?* I would like to let you in on a little secret: it is not a matter of *finding* time, it is simply a matter of *using* the time available. I have the same 24 hours a day available to you, so there is no extra time to locate or find. Rather, it is what I decide to do with the time that is important.

Writing is my passion. I love the creative possibilities of writing, the myriad ways in which I can share my experiences and ideas with readers. I enjoy the opportunities to discover more about the world and to explain those discoveries to others. Writing excites me, gets my senses racing, and is one of the most creative and personally fulfilling activities I know. It is very much a part of who and what I am.

Because it is such an important part of my life, I make sure there is time for writing. I am usually up at 5:30 in the morning, and soon I am at my computer with a cup of coffee on my desk and a few ideas flashing across my computer screen. It is my daily ritual. I spend a minimum of two to three hours writing every day, even on busy days. This time of the morning is *my* time. The dog is by my side, the world outside is quiet, and the birds are just beginning to chirp.

I have found that carving this particular slice out of my day has become a welcomed ritual. Writing is something I do routinely, like tying my shoes, brushing my teeth, or putting on a tie. Because the first two to three hours of the morning are my writing time, my day would seem incomplete if I did not spend that time writing.

It is important to establish personal rituals or routines that we love and enjoy. This gives us a sense of anticipation and completion each day. On those rare occasions when I cannot write in the morning, I feel as though something is missing. That is because I have established that slice of time for *my time*—time I have created and protected from the pressures of everyday life, a gift to myself.

Your pleasure might be reading a novel, working on a quilt, or painting a landscape. Carve out a section of each day and designate it as *your time*. Ask those around you to respect your time and make it available to you.

For Reflection

❧ Plan some *My Time* in your day, every day.

❧ Make your day complete by giving something back to yourself.

❧ Doing something for yourself provides you with increased opportunities to do something for others.

~23~
Who You Want to Be

What concerns me is not the way things are,
but rather the way people think things are.
Epictetus

When I first began to teach, I heard a story I have never forgotten. Many years ago a first-year teacher was given her class list of students and next to each student's name was a number. The teacher assumed that the number reflected each student's IQ. She developed a curriculum that provided a wide range of dynamic and creative activities for students who had large numbers in front of their names. At the same time she designed a series of skill sheets and repetitive activities for those students who had smaller numbers in front of their names. She assumed that students with higher IQs would do better with the creative activities, and students with lower IQs would benefit from the repetitive, skill-oriented activities.

At the end of the school year all the students were tested. Not surprisingly, the students who had been provided with the most creative activities did much better on the standardized tests than did the students who had been given the dull, repetitive activities. When the teacher handed in her grade book on the last day of school, the school secretary told her that the number in front of each student's name was not an IQ score but was each student's locker number.

This is what is known as a self-fulfilling prophecy. This is the phenomenon whereby a person's actions are based on a belief that is false, and his or her actions cause the belief to come true.

Self-fulfilling prophecies can happen to anyone. We may believe ourselves to be deficient in a particular area or unskilled in another. Then we participate in actions and activities that help to make those thoughts or beliefs true—whether or not they are. In short, we seek to confirm our thoughts with our actions.

Self-fulfilling prophecies can create positive outcomes, as well. In fact, top-ranked athletes include this in their training. They create a mental picture of a forthcoming athletic contest, and they picture themselves competing to the best of their ability. Most importantly, they envision themselves winning that contest. They may replay these mental images over and over again. When the actual contest to takes place, the athlete already knows the outcome because he or she has prepared for it.

Take a minute to create your own prophecy. Think about a change you would like to make, a goal you would like to attain, or an attitude you would like to assume. Create a *mental image* and review it again and again. See it; feel it; believe it. In time, you will see yourself accomplishing that task and feeling more confident. You will begin to feel more self-assured. It is a simple mind game, but it makes all the difference.

For Reflection

✤ Have you visualized the person you would like to be?

✤ What are your personal goals? Can you visualize yourself reaching them?

✤ What do you believe about your ability to achieve them?

~24~
Submit an Application to Become a Human Being

Always be a first-rate version of you,
instead of a second-rate version of somebody else.
Judy Garland

When you applied for your first teaching position you probably had to compose a resume or vita. You listed your objectives, your education, your G.P.A., your employment history, your membership in professional organizations, and contact information. Your goal was to obtain that first, all-important teaching position. As a result, you attempted to present your best side; a capsule summary of yourself designed to impress a principal or supervisor.

Let's look at a different kind of resume. Pretend for a moment that you are applying for a position as a human being at a place called the *Human School.* That's right—you are applying to become a member of the human race. What would you list on your resume? What features, qualifications, or talents would you list to secure a job as a fully contributing member of society?

Take a few moments and complete the resume on the next page.

Objective in Life: _____

Personal Education (not formal education): _____

Experiences as a Human: _____

Special Human Skills: _____

Memberships: _____

References: _____

This little exercise can reveal some important human traits. It can allow you to reflect on yourself and your interactions with the larger community of human beings. It can also provide a valuable opportunity to evaluate your growth and development. Take time once a year to create a new resume.

This exercise will not solve all your problems or provide the answers to all of life's questions, but it will allow you precious time to look inward—to take stock of who you are and where you are headed. You may discover some beautiful things about yourself. You may even discover some hidden talents. Best of all, you may discover a very important person in the school of human beings.

For Reflection

❧ What would you like to contribute to humankind?

❧ Would you hire someone like you as a member of the *Human School*?

❧ Do you have all the skills and attributes you would like to see in other members?

❧ Reminder: One's resume should be updated every year or so!

Reflect ~ My Thoughts

Refocus ~ My Goals

Recharge ~ My Actions

What are you already happy with in your personal life?

Where do you see opportunities for change or improvement?

Who might be able to support you?

What will you need in order to achieve this goal?

How will you communicate your needs to others?

What is one simple change you can make to get started?

Relationship
Growth

~25~

Appreciate Those Closest to You

Here is something to think about. If you had to leave school today, and you had just one hour of time before you left, who would you see, and what would you say? Would you spend most of that hour talking with colleagues or friends, saying your last good-byes, and sharing your memories of the times you shared together? What would you say to them?

Although we may never be put in that kind of situation, questions remain. What would you share with friends and colleagues if you had only a short amount of time to express how much you have enjoyed their company, advice, love, and counsel over the years? Would you feel rushed to include everything you would like to say?

My father passed away less than two months after I turned 21. I was on the threshold of adulthood and had lost the opportunity to discuss my dreams and aspirations with my father. I never had the chance to share some of my personal goals with him. Even sadder, I was never able to thank him for the advice and counsel that shaped my life. For many years, I felt that an important part of my life was incomplete because I had not expressed my feelings to someone so important to me.

Here is a simple strategy. Sometime during your day, pretend that you have only one more hour in your current position. Select one person with whom you work—a fellow teacher, the custodian, or a secretary in the office. Tell that person how much you enjoy his or her company, how much he or she is contributing to the lives of students, how much he or she is helping to make the school a good place to work. You do not have to talk face to face—a short note in an in-school mailbox, a phone call at the end of the day, or a letter to a home address is sufficient.

Imagine how the person might feel upon the receiving your message. Imagine how you would feel if you received such a message of appreciation. Your message does not have to be long; it does not have to be complex. Just a simple thank you is enough. You will be surprised at the results.

For Reflection

❧ Make a point to let people know— especially those closest to you—how much you enjoy them, appreciate them, and love them.

❧ Thank one person each day for his or her company.

❧ Appreciate others, and you will receive appreciation in return.

~26~

See Beyond
People's Roles

A good friend of mine, a third-grade teacher in an urban school district, does something that I find very refreshing and very unique. Each morning Sarah mentally identifies one person in her school, perhaps a fellow teacher, a custodian, librarian, secretary, or an administrator, and she designates that individual as her *object of attention* for the day.

During the course of the day, she seeks out that person and spends a few moments talking with him or her. She may drop a note on the person's desk when she arrives in the morning. She may offer to buy the individual a cup of coffee for an after school conversation. She may send the person a thank you note for something he or she did for her or for the school. Or, she may make it a point to sit next to that person at lunch and strike up a conversation. She makes a conscious effort to give that person some extra attention, just as she would do with a good friend.

Sarah tells me that this routine has given a new purpose to each day. It helps her get to know many different people in the school—people she may not have discovered otherwise. She discovered that she and the gym teacher share the same love of travel. She found out that one of the custodians collects stamps, just as her father does. She learned that her parents and those of the school secretary went to the same school together.

Sarah says that this little exercise has revealed the personalities of people, more than the jobs they hold. She says, *I no longer think of Robert, the custodian, as someone who simply empties my trash can in the afternoon, but as someone who shares the same hobby as my father. It has helped me move beyond job descriptions and into the real lives and personalities of the people I work with.*

In the hierarchy of school positions, it is easy to cluster people into job roles: *She is the instructional aide, He is the reading specialist, She is the receptionist,* and so on. It is important to look beyond job responsibilities and see the person behind these roles. What do you know about the lives of the people with whom you work? Making a conscious effort to learn a little about those we work with helps us learn more about ourselves. It can also result in a little more peace and harmony in our lives.

For Reflection

&? Get to know the people behind the roles at your school. You may discover some interesting new information and make some interesting new friends.

&? Look beyond the job that someone does and get to know him or her as a person.

&? Create opportunities to associate with people other than teachers.

~27~
Give the Other Guy the Right to Be Wrong

My father was a corporate attorney. He had an office high in the United California Bank building in Beverly Hills. Over the years he tried many cases, large and small. Many he won, and though as a child I found it hard to believe, he lost a few, too.

My father taught me something important. He used to tell me, *Give the other guy the right to be wrong.* For the longest time, I found this difficult to accept. I wondered if I had misunderstood his words. But as I got older and began to interact with more and more people, I began to see the wisdom of his words.

Like you, occasionally I have fallen into the trap of believing that I know what is best for other people. Let's face it—I am a teacher; I have been trained to help improve the lives of others. I chose a profession that is dedicated to assisting others educationally, emotionally, and socially.

However, I have grown to realize that I am not the master of anyone else's life. I do not have all the answers, and I have a full-time job dealing with my own goals and aspirations. I can only make decisions for me; I cannot make them for anyone else.

Allowing others to be wrong requires a great deal of patience and self-restraint. Whenever I take charge and tell someone that he or she is wrong, I am expecting that person to live life according to my standards. That is not fair. None of us has all of the solutions and answers for another person's life. Allowing others to work through their own problems provides them the satisfaction of discovering the solutions for themselves. Our individual freedom to be wrong is far better than the need to be right, as dictated by another.

I must admit that I still wrestle with my father's words. But they have given me pause to gain a new perspective. I often discover that the *wrongs* of a person can sometimes be endearing qualities. To be honest, I really do not know what I would do if I ever met a perfect person. Do you?

For Reflection

&c People have the right to be wrong, just as much as they have the right to be correct.

&c We may not always know what is best for others.

&c If it is true that we learn from our mistakes, doesn't that hold true for others as well?

&c Correcting others' mistakes takes time away from attending to our own imperfections and mistakes.

~28~

Look at the Whole Person

My wife and I live out in the country, surrounded by woods and trees. We enjoy hanging many bird feeders around our house to attract a variety of feathered friends. Attached to the railing of our deck, just outside the sliding glass door to our kitchen is the large feeder that creatures visit most.

This particular feeder is filled with a mixture of birdseed—cracked corn, thistle seed, sunflower seed, and the like to attract the widest variety of bird life that we can. But this smorgasbord also attracts other creatures, namely squirrels.

We do not chase the squirrels away; they are infrequent visitors, and we enjoy watching their antics as they scamper up to the feeder to nibble at the goodies. But squirrels, like many species of birds, are specific eaters. They only enjoy the sunflower seeds. They sweep aside all the other seeds just to get at a few sunflower seeds. They paw at the seeds, disperse them in all directions, capture one or two sunflower seeds in their paws, and sit there munching away. After they have had their fill of sunflower seeds, they scoot away, leaving scattered seeds all over the deck and spread on the ground below.

I suspect that, as teachers, we occasionally act like squirrels. We sometimes regard our students as a squirrel might view a mixture of seeds. We tend to focus on selected characteristics of students. Sometimes we fail to recognize that each individual has a range of qualities. We certainly recognize that each individual is unique and has a distinctive personality, but too often we reduce our focus to a single trait or attribute.

In the past, I know I have been guilty of assigning a temporary label to an individual child. I would often say that a student was a problem child while ignoring the fact that she had completed a complicated young adult novel or earned a special badge in scouting. I have tagged a student as a remedial reader while bypassing his accomplishments on the baseball team or his music performance. In this way, I have behaved as the squirrels at my bird feeder do.

Labels are easy and convenient. However, labels do not take into account the range of attributes and attitudes of the individual. They isolate one factor, often a negative factor, and disregard the totality of the person.

Be careful not to categorize or label people, especially your students. In so doing, we neglect the whole person for the sake of convenience. The completed puzzle is more interesting than just a few isolated pieces.

For Reflection

🐾 Are you able to see the complete child in every student?

🐾 Are you able to see the whole person in every colleague?

🐾 Be careful about assigning labels; they may place people in categories from which they may never escape.

🐾 What are the attributes you admire in people? Are you able to celebrate those attributes in those you do not know as well?

~29~

You're in Control

No one has the right to determine
what kind of day I'm going to have.
Eleanor Roosevelt

Several years ago I taught with a person who was perpetually grouchy. She would arrive at school in a bad mood, sustain a bad mood throughout the day, and leave school in the same bad mood in which she arrived. She would complain about the principal, the school board, the parents, the secretary, the custodian, and any other person that came to mind. She was a permanent sourpuss. Frankly, I cannot remember a single time she smiled, told a joke, or seemed to enjoy anything.

It was very difficult being in this person's presence. Her negativity seemed to be contagious. She could put a damper on almost any activity, from lunch in the teacher's lounge, to a workshop, to bus duty on a warm sunny day. She embodied the word *grouch* for everyone in the school.

We can allow other people to influence our moods or our approach to life. If we walk into a supermarket, and the cashier is grumpy, the bagger is rushed, and the manager is stressed, we can take on those moods. Conversely, if we arrive at school, and the secretary is humming, the custodian is whistling, and our closest friend just received some good news, we too, assume those attitudes. Our attitude or outlook is often reflective of those around us.

One of the greatest lessons I have learned is embodied in the Eleanor Roosevelt quote. It reminds me that I alone determine the type of day I have. When I leap out of bed in the morning in a good mood, I make the decision that I will be in a good mood for the rest of the day, regardless of the grouches or grumps I may meet along the way. In others words, I decide what my frame of mind will be for the day; that decision will not be made for me by anyone else. I maintain control over my day and how I will approach it. It is a personal, individual choice I make, and one that keeps me focused on the events before me, not a decision arbitrarily imposed on me by others.

For Reflection

✿ Make up your mind that today's success is determined by you.

✿ Wake up with the thought that this day will be your day.

✿ Don't let the complainers get you down. Their unhappiness belongs to them, not to you.

✿ Smile at a grouch—something good may happen.

~30~
"May I Hold Your Hand?"

As a children's author, I spend a lot of travel time in airports. Several years ago I was flying from Chicago to Harrisburg, Pennsylvania, following a long and satisfying day of presentations in an Illinois school district. I boarded the plane, located my seat on the aisle, and began to settle in for the flight home.

Sitting in the window seat next to me was a young woman about 25 years old. She secured her seatbelt and pulled the safety card from the seat pocket in front of her to read and reread several times. Time after time she glanced out the window, and it became obvious that she was extremely nervous. I asked her if this was her first flight, and she said it was. As we began a conversation, she told me that she was flying to Pennsylvania to spend some time with her fiancé over the approaching holiday.

Closer to flight time, she became even more unsettled. The flight attendant reviewed the pre-flight instructions, and the plane taxied onto the runway. My companion was even more anxious than before. As the engines revved up, she turned and asked me a question: *I'm really scared. May I hold your hand?*

For the first five minutes of our flight, I held hands with a stranger. She squeezed my hand tightly as the plane took off. The scenario was repeated prior to our landing. Once again, she asked if she could hold my hand, and she did so until the plane taxied up to the gate. While retrieving my luggage, I saw her arm-in-arm with her fiancé. She caught my eye and smiled, and the two of them strolled out of the baggage claim area.

The experience touched me in many ways. Most importantly, it reminded me that when we do something for the first time—drive a car, start a job, fly in an airplane—it is scary. This is also true for children. Learning how to read for the first time can be a scary experience. Learning the multiplication tables can be overwhelming for some students. Learning how to use a microscope can be a complex task for many students. Learning is a partnership between someone who is proficient in an area and someone who is less proficient at that task. It requires a bond of mutual respect, as well as a bond of support and encouragement. A student, just like a first-time airline passenger, frequently needs someone beside him or her who is willing to provide support. He or she needs someone who is willing to hold his or her hand.

Although I do not make it a practice to hold the hand of the person sitting beside me, when I fly I try to remember that there may be passengers who have never experienced air travel. I try to be aware that there may be children who have never listened to a book read aloud, never constructed a diorama, or never participated in a skit. One of the best things we can do is to *hold their hands* during the learning process. We may begin the journey as strangers, but we become partners as we reach our destination.

For Reflection

&& Remember that learning is a mutual partnership.

&& We often learn best when there is someone by our side.

&& Hold hands with others—physically and mentally.

~31~
Take a Few Extra Minutes to Be Polite

I may be a little old-fashioned, but I have always believed that the three most important words in the English language are *Please* and *Thank you*. I do not mean to be stodgy, but I think we sometimes forget to use those words enough.

On my way to work the other day, I stopped at my local donut shop for a cup of coffee and a donut. There were several people ahead of me in line. Each customer would bark an order to the person behind the counter who would pour the coffee and gather the requested flavor of donut. *Gimmee two glazed donuts and a coffee light,* the customer would shout, then hand over the money, grab the waiting bag, and head out the door. There was little exchange of conversation, and neither the customers nor the young woman behind the counter ever made eye contact or engaged in any conversation.

Approaching the counter, I asked, *Could you please pour me a cup of black coffee? I would also like a glazed donut.* Her expression revealed a hint of surprise as she filled my request in short order. I handed her my money, and while she made change, I thanked her for helping me. She smiled and said, *Do you know you are the first person this morning to say thank you. That's really nice.* Her smile lingered as I left the shop.

To be certain, we live in a fast-paced world, but not so fast-paced that we cannot take a moment to show our appreciation for the other people we encounter each day. The waitress who brings your food order to the table, the mechanic who orders a special part for your car, the clerk in the bookstore, the attendant at the gym, and the person who delivers your newspaper all deserve recognition and appreciation.

I have sometimes found that simply adding *Please* when I order food in a restaurant or ask for assistance in my local garden shop results in better service. By the same token, I have discovered that a *Thank you* at the conclusion of a transaction results in a smile from the recipient. It is a way of communicating our respect for our fellow human beings. I think *Please* and *Thank you* are the best forms of communication. There is no substitute for courtesy.

For Reflection

❧ Don't forget the three most magical words in the English language. Use them regularly.

❧ Put some magic in someone's life with courtesy.

❧ Everybody deserves recognition and respect. Show that you care.

~32~
Give Someone a Hug

Several years ago I came across a quotation in a back issue of *Reader's Digest* that has had an influence on my life. It goes like this: *A hug is the perfect gift—one size fits all, and nobody minds if you exchange it.*

When was the last time you gave someone a hug? Was it yesterday, last week, some time ago? Do you really have to think about it to remember?

I believe that hugs come in two forms—physical hugs and verbal hugs. Now, allow me to ask the question again. When was the last time you gave someone a hug—either a physical one or a verbal one?

Our lives seem so hectic that we do not give enough hugs, especially to those we truly care about. We may say things like, *Of course, he knows how much I love him,* or *I only give hugs for really special occasions.* We may think of hugs as a special token of affection, not realizing that they are an essential part of every relationship.

I am an early riser and like nothing better than getting up at 5:30 in the morning, fixing a strong cup of coffee, and sitting at my desk to continue writing a children's book or to initiate some research on a new teacher resource. That is a special time for me, my most creative time of the day.

My wife, on the other hand, is definitely not a morning person. She prefers to sleep late and begin her day at 9:00AM or

10:00AM, a time I consider the middle of the afternoon. It is quite obvious that our personal time clocks are set to different schedules.

However, there is one routine that is an important part of every day for both of us. As soon as she has completed her morning routine, she comes into my office. I stop whatever I am working on, and we share a meaningful embrace. We share an affectionate moment and some of our thoughts for the day. We both look forward to this time together, and we find that it is a wonderful way to start the day.

Hugging those who are important in your life—a spouse, a friend, your children—is both expressive and sustaining. Think of a hug, either physical or verbal, as a way of becoming closer with another human being. It is fun, it is genuine comfort, and it fosters strong bonds of affection and communication.

What more could you ask for in life?

For Reflection

❧ Share a hug. You may get one in return.

❧ Distribute hugs frequently and randomly throughout your day—and throughout your life.

❧ It's very difficult to be unhappy when you give someone a hug.

~33~
Make Smiling a Regular Part of Your Day

Several years ago there was a song with the title *Don't Worry, Be Happy!* While this was a simplistic way at looking at life, the beat and melody of that song could be heard in every elevator, store, restaurant, and mall throughout the country for months. Everybody was greeting everybody else with the title to the song, and it became a mantra for thousands of people.

The song also conjured up an exercise that can be very instructive, particularly for teachers. It is a strategy I use quite frequently, and it helps me appreciate the positive points of my job and my day. In fact, it is one of the simplest exercises in this book, and one of the most rewarding.

When was the last time you smiled? Think about that question. Do you have trouble coming up with a response? Is it difficult to remember the last time you smiled? What was it, exactly, that made you smile?

This strategy involves nothing more complicated than a few moments; a small spiral-bound notepad and a pen or pencil. Keep the notepad on your nightstand next to your bed. Each evening as you retire, try to think of one thing that made you smile that day. Record that event in your notebook. Do this each and every day. To help me remember, I write the day's date at the top of a page in the notebook when I rise in the morning. In the evening, I record a positive event. The next day I repeat the cycle.

This exercise helps me focus on the positive aspects of my daily life. It reminds me that there will be at least one smile each day—a smile to be recorded and remembered. Day by day, it validates my knowledge that joy exists, no matter where I teach or how long I have been teaching.

On those days when everything seems to pile up, I can sit down on the side of the bed and read selected pages from my ongoing notepad. The passages remind me of the joyous parts of my job. The notepad is a glorious reminder of the smiles that are so much a part of our profession.

Many years ago my wife asked me what I find most attractive in a woman. I said, *Her smile. The most beautiful part of a woman is her smile. Yes, it was your smile that first attracted me to you,* I said. She and I have been smiling for more than 30 years now!

For Reflection

⁂ What makes you happy? Record it, and practice it.

⁂ Take time during your day to write down the little things that make you smile. Look back on these writings and smile all over again.

⁂ Share a smile with yourself or share a smile with a friend. You'll see some magical things begin to happen.

⁂ An accumulation of smiles is a celebration of the good in life.

~34~
Tell Them How Much You Love Them

Live with your family—not your job.
Gizz Davis, retired teacher, York, PA

This next strategy is a challenging one, so be prepared! In the left-hand column of the table below, write the names of several people you care about. Be sure to include your spouse, your children, your parents, your relatives, your students, your friends, and your colleagues. Do that first.

1. _____   _____
2. _____   _____
3. _____   _____
4. _____   _____
5. _____   _____
6. _____   _____
7. _____   _____
8. _____   _____
9. _____   _____
10. _____   _____

Now the challenging part. In the second column, record the last time you did something for each individual listed in the first column. Be sure that you are writing about something that showed that you really cared for them.

It is sad, but in our fast-paced world of email, cell phones, and other communication aids, we do not stop to tell the people closest to us how much we care about them. It is easy to pick up our cell phone and make a dentist appointment. But how much more meaningful it would be to pick up a pen a write a note to a child you love. It is so much easier to participate in a chat room with people whom you have never met than it is to buy a greeting card for a friend or parent.

It is easy to take for granted those who mean the most to us. We assume they will always be there, and we know they will always love us. They will stick by us through thick and thin. Isn't that all the more reason to take a few minutes out of our day to call, write, or send them something that shows we appreciate them?

Carve some time out of your day to tell someone how much you care. A phone call, a note, a letter, a message, a greeting card, or even a simple hug will bring something special into that person's life, as well as your own.

For Reflection

❧ When was the last time you told someone that you loved them?

❧ Be careful that you don't take those closest to you for granted.

❧ Complete the lives of those you love, and your life will be complete.

~35~
Share a
Little Sunshine

I spend a lot of time at the post office buying stamps, sending out manuscripts, and picking up packages. The other day I walked into our local post office, and the young lady behind the counter said, *Oh, here comes our favorite customer!* I looked at her somewhat bewildered and asked, *What do you mean 'favorite customer'?* She replied, *Every time you come in here you are always singing or whistling. You always seem to bring some sunshine with you!*

I was delighted to hear that, to say the least. But it also got me thinking about how often service people such as postal clerks, cashiers, waitresses, custodians, and so on, have to interact with grumpy, sad, grouchy, or just plain difficult people during the course of their work day. They regularly have to listen to tirades, complaints, short tempers, and other less-than-pleasant comments from the public. It must wear thin after a while.

Bringing a little sunshine into the lives of others is a pleasurable and rewarding experience. People who deal with complaints, special requests, and demands on their time are particularly deserving of a simple acknowledgement or friendly greeting. Anyone who copes with the demands of daily living is entitled to a pleasant hello. Spreading a little joy is a simple act, but it is more than an attitude. It is more than simple courtesy. It is also a belief—a belief that we can positively influence other people through simple words and actions.

For Reflection

- Sing a song.
- Whistle a tune.
- Share a smile.
- Now, watch what happens!

~36~
Do Something Unexpected

One of our favorite travel destinations is Hawaii. My wife and I love traveling to the islands to walk in the tropical landscape, stroll down a quiet beach, and drive along a winding road to the top of an extinct volcano, or talk with native islanders at a fruit stand along the side of the road. The constant sunshine, exquisite food, and aloha spirit of the people of Hawaii draw us back again and again. More than a romantic paradise, Hawaii is also a spiritual paradise.

Imagine my surprise when I walked in the door a few months ago to find that my wife had turned the dining room into a temporary Hawaiian paradise. Paper orchids were blooming in the corners of the room, Hawaiian music was playing on the stereo, my wife was dressed in her favorite Hawaiian dress, and a tropical feast was laid out on the table.

What's this? I asked in surprise. She replied that because it had been a while since our last trip to the islands, she thought I might enjoy a surprise journey to Hawaii. Although our travel was limited to our dining room in Pennsylvania, I changed into my aloha shirt and souvenir flower lei. My wife and I enjoyed our memories of the spirit of the islands. That unexpected luau was a tonic for the soul.

Too often we go through our days in a kind of stupor. As teachers, we have routines that we tend to follow day after day. We often know what to expect and just go through the motions. One day is almost like every other day.

A wonderful way to break up the sameness of our daily routines is to do something unexpected for someone else. Arrive early and leave a flower on someone's desk. Offer to write a lesson for a colleague. Stop by the library and pick up some books for someone who is ill. Offer to cover the phones for the school secretary so she can take an extended lunch break. Small offerings of time and effort can refresh the spirit and renew the soul. What matters most is that we share a little of ourselves with someone and offer a welcomed break from the routine.

Luau, anyone?

For Reflection

❧ Do something unexpected for someone today.

❧ Help others break up their routine, and it will help break up yours, too.

❧ Reducing the stress of others can help reduce yours as well.

~37~
Celebrate Importance

Education is not the filling of a pail,
but the lighting of a fire.
William Butler Yeats

What do you like about your closest friend? What qualities do you like about yourself? Your answer to these two questions can provide powerful insight into what drives you and what sustains you as an individual. Let's take a look.

Pretend to write a letter to a friend (no email—you want the sensation of putting pen to paper). In your letter tell your friend what you like most about him or her. Is it a sense of humor, an ability to tackle difficult challenges, tenacity, or willingness to help? Whatever it is you admire in that person, write it down and provide one or two examples. Specifically compliment the individual for her or his special qualities.

Now, reverse the process and write a letter to yourself. What do you admire about yourself? Do you have a special skill or trait that others enjoy, do you evidence a special talent in the classroom, is there a particular aspect of your personality that is noteworthy? Whatever they are, write them down. Congratulate yourself on your ability to influence others in your special way.

This exercise can have powerful benefits. On one level, you will discover how you are similar to a friend or colleague you admire. On another level, you will begin to examine admirable traits in yourself. I am not suggesting that we ignore the fine qualities of our friends and colleagues, but it is important for us to recognize and celebrate our own worthwhile abilities, attitudes, and outlook.

Put each of these letters into a separate envelope and stamp them. Address one to your friend and one to yourself. Drop them in the mail. When your letter arrives, take a few moments to review it and pat yourself on the back. Congratulate yourself in some way. Then, write two more letters, one to another friend and another one to yourself.

This may seem a little time consuming, but it is worthwhile. It celebrates your importance within the human experience and honors the qualities you admire most in others. I think you will discover, as I did, that you gain increased awareness of the positive qualities you enjoy in others in addition to those you discover about yourself. You will have the opportunity to congratulate two very important people.

For Reflection

❧ Think about what you like about yourself and celebrate it.

❧ Take time to recognize the importance of a friend. Let her or him know about your thoughts.

❧ "Shake hands" with yourself on a regular basis.

❧ Congratulate yourself on who you are, as well as who you will become.

~38~

Practice Sharing Compliments

Do you remember the last time someone paid you a compliment—sincere, heartfelt words of praise? When was the last time someone said how much he or she enjoys your company, how much he or she likes what you are doing in the classroom, or how much he or she appreciates a lesson or project you created for your students? Do you wait for those compliments?

When was the last time you paid a friend or colleague a sincere compliment? Was it today? Was it yesterday? Was it last week? Do you even remember?

If there is one thing I have discovered about this great and noble profession of ours, it is that genuine compliments beget respect. That is to say, the more time we spend in recognizing and celebrating the accomplishments of others, the more they will acknowledge and applaud our work, too. Teaching professionals can create a mutual admiration society.

All of us enjoy receiving the accolades of our peers. The recognition of others is an important part of who we are and how we view ourselves. It is also important for us to regularly celebrate the accomplishments of those with whom we live and work. Did someone make an unhappy child laugh? Did a colleague tackle a demanding chore that was avoided by everyone else? Did a supervisor provide you with materials for an upcoming lesson?

It is not important that we actively seek out reciprocal compliments. The important fact is that when people around us are appreciated and feel genuinely valued for the things they do, they invest greater effort and energy in their jobs. We do not give praise in order to seek praise. Rather, we recognize the efforts of others to show them that they are valued. In so doing, they feel a greater sense of personal satisfaction, and commitment to continued success.

We praise our students, not so that they will compliment us in return, but so that they might be encouraged to do better on ensuing tasks. The same perspective can be an important part of the relationship we have with our colleagues as well.

For Reflection

❧ Do you regularly celebrate the accomplishments of others?

❧ Take time each day to reward others for the work they do—you may get something in return.

❧ The three best actions the human hand is capable of are a handshake, a hug, and a pat on the back.

❧ Admire and celebrate the work of a colleague. You will make two people happy.

~39~

Think Outside of Stereotypical Roles

Here is an unusual exercise! Read only the first paragraph of this essay, then close the book, and complete the activity. When finished, open the book again, and read the rest of this selection.

Your activity: Draw a picture of a scientist on a blank sheet of paper with a pen or pencil. Close the book and begin.

Finished? Welcome back. I would like to invite you to look closely at your picture of the scientist. How many of the following features or characteristics are included in your illustration? Did you draw a male figure, a lab coat, glasses, a pocket protector filled with pens and pencils, frizzy hair, nerdy clothes, and is the figure is looking in a microscope or working at a lab table?

If you are like most people, you have included several of these features in your illustration. That is because most of us have stereotypes about scientists. We envision most scientists as males. Most scientists work in laboratories. Most scientists wear lab coats and glasses, and have frizzy hair. This is called the Einstein syndrome.

Maybe your diagram is a little different. Maybe you drew a female figure in an open field, in outer space, or underwater. Perhaps your figure was a young child or a teenager holding a butterfly net, an ice pick, or binoculars. If so, your illustration was in the minority. I have assigned this exercise to students as young as first grade and to seasoned graduate students, and more than 90 percent of the time the results reflected stereotypes.

We do this often in our daily lives; we perceive people in stereotypical roles, and we only interact with them in those roles. When I was growing up, I envisioned all school principals as males, dressed in coats and ties. Principals were authoritative, unsmiling, strict disciplinarians. Imagine my surprise when a new female principal began working at a neighboring school. It took me a long time to adjust my thinking.

It is easy to create stereotypes. We assign selected stereotypical roles either to protect ourselves from getting to know a person better or to prevent us from recognizing the various aspects of others. We fail to discover that the principal is a member of the local art association, the custodian is a judo instructor at the YMCA, and the secretary is a long distance runner. One of my friends is a whiz at crossword puzzles and a master of strategy games. He is also a school bus driver for a local school district. I have yet to beat him in a game of chess.

Looking past stereotypes helps us move past the occupational label to learn about the person. A person is not a job description, but an individual with skills, interests, and hobbies–often far more interesting than what they do during their work day.

For Reflection

❧ Do you tend to see people in terms of their roles rather than as real people with lives beyond the workplace?

❧ Do you use stereotypes to *protect* yourself from getting to know someone?

❧ Give others the opportunity to get to know you, too.

~40~

Your Place in the Larger Community

Teaching can be a very isolating profession. A typical school day does not allow teachers a great deal of time for interaction with other adults. Most of our time is spent alone in the classroom with students. Nearly every minute of our workday is spent within the four walls of our own little world.

It is easy to get caught up in the demands of the teaching day. Our schedules often take time away from those periods of time that we need to reassess and reconnect with the world around us. Many of us get into the habit of working through lunch, for example. We stop going to the faculty room, or we rush through the lunch line to grab an apple or a quick salad and head right back to our classrooms. What we may accomplish in that short period of time often does not make up for what we miss.

Although we may enjoy the many opportunities we have to interact with students, it is important to interact with adults. Unstructured and informal situations with colleagues are particularly important. We are so busy trying to foster a sense of community in our classrooms that we forget to maintain our membership in the community *outside* the classroom. Teachers need to share ideas, debate, laugh, and commiserate with other staff members. Our commitment to setting aside this time is necessary to our professional growth and sanity.

Allow yourself time to interact with adults in your school community. Start a book club; talk over a cup of morning coffee; meet for supper once in a while. Get together with colleagues to see a movie, to volunteer, or just to talk about things other than school. Join the community choir, a theater group, a bowling league; join the adult community.

The best reason to take time to interact with the adult community is that it helps us maintain a sense of equilibrium in our lives. It reinforces our understanding that a community is composed of many different members, all working in concert. Maintaining our place in that larger community is an act of maintaining the wholesomeness of the entire community, and of maintaining wholesomeness in our lives.

For Reflection

🌿 Plan regular daily opportunities to interact with the adults in your community.

🌿 Plan informal gatherings and social occasions where you can talk about matters unrelated to teaching.

🌿 Take time after school to communicate with others in a variety of venues. Talk about life, not just about teaching.

~41~
Build a Better Community

Take a few minutes and make a list of all the adults in your school—yes, everyone. Include all of the teachers, the secretaries and custodians, the principal, the reading specialist, the librarian, and the gym teacher—everyone. Now, place a check mark in front of the name of each person with whom you communicated during the course of the past week. Check off everyone you conversed with during the last seven days. Do you see any gaps? Are there people on that list with whom you did not interact? Undoubtedly, you will find that there are some individuals with whom you did not talk last week or maybe not for several weeks in a row.

As classroom teachers, it is quite easy for us to go into our respective classrooms and teach for the entire day without seeing another adult. Obviously, our first and primary responsibility is to instruct our students, and it is easy to forget about all the supportive people who help the school function. In many ways, a school is like a miniature neighborhood with houses (class-rooms), families (students and teachers), a park (playground), a library (library), and other support services.

It is equally important to take the time to recognize that the community we call *school* would not exist or survive without the work and dedication of many individuals. Shouldn't we celebrate the work of all members of our community? I think so.

The next time you are walking through the halls of your school, take a moment to greet a fellow employee. Talk about the weather, the success of the local sports team, children or grandchildren. It does not matter what the conversation is about. Rather, it matters that you take the opportunity to share your time with someone else. Move beyond the simple *Hi, how are you?* greetings we exchange with one another as we rush through the day. Take a minute or two for a brief conversation or a friendly talk. You may discover something interesting. You may discover a kindred spirit.

For Reflection

❧ Begin a conversation with someone new today.

❧ Become someone's friend, not because you have to, but because you want to.

❧ Ask yourself, *Whom don't I know in my school?* Think about your answer.

❧ Ask yourself, *What am I doing to create a cooperative community?*

~42~
Pass Along the Compliments

The other day, I was talking with a group of friends. One of my colleagues said, *You know, I was passing by Bonnie's classroom yesterday, and she sure had those kids excited about that lesson on amphibians.* A few days later I bumped into Bonnie and passed along the comment from my friend, and she grinned from ear to ear. At the end of the day she came back to see me and said, *You know, that comment just made all the difference in my day. I had a tough math lesson to teach, but when I thought about the comment Dave made, it just filled me with such joy.*

We know that teaching is a tough job, and there is too little positive reinforcement. Too many times it seems as though we are taken for granted by our colleagues, administrators, parents, or students. Like our students, we too need an occasional pat on the back.

Whenever I hear something positive about a teaching colleague, I like to pass it along. If I hear a student or teacher say something nice about another person, I try to seek out that person and pass along the comment. You would not believe how much this simple act does to a person's state of mind or ego. Not only does it make the recipient feel valued, it forms the basis of communication between two people. It is not unusual for the recipient to seek out the person who generated the remark and begin a heartfelt dialogue.

I believe it is an important part of the teaching profession for us to be supportive of each other. We should recognize the accomplishments of our colleagues and celebrate those achievements throughout the year. By simply passing along a kind remark, a genuine compliment, or a word of praise, we are helping to establish a community of co-workers that is both supportive and celebratory.

For Reflection

🦋 Solicit praise and comments from others. Share them with your colleagues.

🦋 Be sure to let others know how important they are to the school community.

🦋 Celebrate the good work that people are doing in your school.

🦋 Create praise and pass it along.

Reflect ~ My Thoughts

Refocus ~ My Goals

Recharge ~ My Actions

What are you already happy with in your relationships?

Where do you see opportunities for change or improvement?

Who might be able to support you?

What will you need in order to achieve this goal?

How will you communicate your needs to others?

What is one simple change you can make to get started?

Professional Growth

~43~
Drive Home a Different Way

Here's a simple strategy that can work wonders; drive home a different way.

When I first heard this idea from a friend, I didn't believe it. It sounded too simple. How could it make a difference in my day? My friend, ever patient, just said, *Try it for a week, and you will see a big difference.*

For the next week I drove home a different way each time. I took a different route to work each morning, too. Yes, it made a difference, a tremendous difference.

I know my usual route to work like I know the back of my own hand. I know exactly how many traffic signals I will encounter, how many grocery stores I will pass, how many corner churches along the way, and the locations of all of the gas stations. Without thinking, I can get in my car, put it in gear, and drive to my destination in exactly 25 minutes.

The problem with that drive, I discovered, was that it had become a routine. Since I did not have to think about where I was going or what I was seeing, I tended to focus on the things that were consuming my thoughts—a new lesson plan I wanted to try, students I needed to conference with, a report I had to write. As I maneuvered the car by automatic pilot, my mind was occupied with the causes of my stress. In short, I brought my work with me into the car, extending my workday on both ends.

When I began to travel by a new route to work, I was able to focus on the aspects of the ride. I saw a row of houses I had never noticed before. I observed a pair of cyclists traveling down the road. I found an old barn that was rotting and falling apart. I saw a For Sale sign on a house that looked interesting from the road. I discovered a herd of cattle silently grazing by a small pond. My mind focused on new discoveries.

I discovered that new routes were a tonic for my thoughts. Instead of focusing on the challenges of my day, I now had the opportunity to focus on new aspects of my world. This became a sort of mental cleansing, a way of focusing on items, objects, and scenery that were not part of my workday and a way of separating my workday from my environment. The result was that I arrived at my destination more refreshed and better able to tackle the tasks ahead.

For Reflection

❧ Plan a new route home today. Look for new discoveries and new adventures.

❧ Make the day different, and you will begin to see things differently. Every day will be fresh and adventurous.

❧ Break routines and break habits. The result is growth.

❧ On your way home, stop for an ice cream cone and pull off onto the side of the road. Observe.

~44~
Membership in a Group

My wife belongs to a small group of local women artists called Third Tuesday. Each month they meet to critique and discuss each other's work and to study one another as artists. They examine each other's work in order to observe the imprint of the artist behind the art. If a member is straying from her true self, the group gently nudges her back. These meetings are not so much about art as they are about life. The members share a common passion, and they have created a common bond.

Two members of the group are high-powered, energetic women. Their husbands are retired, and they are involved in a wide variety of civic and local responsibilities. They are well loved and respected members of the community and of their group. They are both talented artists, and they both have cancer.

One woman has breast cancer and has undergone an intensive series of chemotherapy, radiation treatments, and a mastectomy. The other woman is dealing with pancreatic cancer. She has seen a series of specialists, has undergone massive doses of chemotherapy, and has been subjected to an intense regimen of radiation therapy. Both women are facing the cruelest and most insidious of diseases, and both are facing their challenges with strength and determination.

Supportive families sustain both women in their battles. Perhaps as important, they are nurtured and strengthened by their membership in Third Tuesday. The group was conceived and established as an opportunity for members to grow professionally, to expand their creative horizons, and to spread their artistic wings. All are successful artists and have established themselves at the local and regional levels, but these women are much more than artists.

The two members' battles with cancer find the support of friends in the Tuesday group. They are buoyed by the humor, sustained by the camaraderie, and strengthened by a common bond of love and admiration. Both women are embracing life and holding on, unwilling to flinch or to succumb. The once-a-month meetings with Third Tuesday renew their hope, drive, and resolve.

Often we join professional groups to obtain new ideas, seek fellowship, or to provide a creative outlet for our work. Good groups reach far beyond those parameters to transcend the dictates of a profession, hobby, or skill. They sustain the soul and elevate the mind. The group's purpose becomes secondary to the soul of each individual within the group. The celebration of people is more valuable than the attainment of a professional objective.

Open your eyes to learning more about the people within a group, and you may see more than goals and objectives. You will discover heart and spirit.

For Reflection

❧ Join a group, one that has nothing to do with institutionalized education.

❧ Find a group that nurtures your spirit and the soul, not just your mind.

❧ Seek camaraderie and embrace friendship through varied memberships.

❧ Look beyond the roles and into the hearts of the group members

~45~
Discover Something New

View yourself as a facilitator and as a learner.
When you think you have all the answers, you're in trouble.
Stef Crumbling, fourth-grade teacher, York, PA

When was the last time you made a discovery? I am not referring to setting foot on a new land or coming up with a cure for the common cold. I am referring to a common, everyday, run-of-the-mill discovery—something you found or learned that was unknown.

Our house sits in the middle of a four-acre tract of land filled with trees. We have discovered a small trail through those woods that winds beside a small stream that cuts across the corner of the property. The trail winds across a short field of boulders, up the side of a gentle slope, and ends at the edge of the backyard.

My dog and I like to explore that trail every so often. I usually set out wondering, *What can we discover today?* I never know what new sight, unusual creature, or interesting discovery we may encounter. Sienna and I simply set out to see what we can find.

One time Sienna and I were sauntering down the trail when she began to dig under an old rotting log. Wanting to see what she was pawing at, I got down on my hands and knees to have a look. There was enormous nest of oversized termites—

termites that I had never seen before. I was fascinated to discover these creatures, and the two of us spent about 15 minutes observing them.

Although finding termites might not rank very high on your list of new discoveries, I am suggesting that setting out to discover something new once in a while can add zest to your day. Your goal may be to discover some new ability in one of your students, a new aspect of a colleague's personality, a new route home, a new flavor at the local ice cream stand, or even a nest of termites. What is important is that the potential for discovery is all around us. Our lives are refreshed and renewed when we make a conscious effort to look for the *new* in our lives.

I have found that I am more aware of the people and places around me when I set a personal discovery goal. I may record my discovery in my diary under *What would I like to discover today?* My goal is to learn more about my environment and about the people around me. I am revitalized by knowing that there is something new, something undiscovered out there for me to find. Putting on the explorer's hat can be an exciting experience and can help us renew our sense of adventure.

For Reflection

✤ Make one new discovery every day.

✤ Be an explorer of life.

✤ Look for the new, different, and unusual.

✤ Celebrate adventure.

~46~
Problems as Opportunities

My sister sent me the following story via email the other day. I do not know who originated the story since it had been forwarded through many other people. I would dearly like to give credit to someone for composing this tale but am unable to do so. However, I would like to share it with you since it has much to say about our roles as teachers as well as our roles as human beings.

> In ancient times, a King had a boulder placed in the middle of a roadway by one of his servants. The King hid himself and watched to see how travelers would react to the huge obstacle. Some of the king's wealthiest merchants and courtiers came down the road and simply walked around the boulder. Many loudly blamed the king for not keeping the roads clear, but no one did anything to move the boulder out of the way. A peasant came along carrying a load of vegetables. Upon approaching the boulder, the peasant laid down his burden and tried to move it to the side of the road. After much pushing and straining, he finally succeeded. Upon picking up his load of vegetables, the peasant noticed a purse lying in

the road where the boulder had been. The purse contained many gold coins and a note from the king indicating that the gold was a gift for the person who removed the boulder from the roadway. The peasant learned something that people seldom realize. Every obstacle presents an opportunity to improve our condition.

Perceiving problems as opportunities, rather than as barriers, can be a refreshing way to deal with challenges. If you look ahead and see a road full of immovable boulders, you will feel discouraged. You may be reluctant to face the journey or feel paralyzed by negativity. However, if you view potential challenges as learning opportunities, you can approach the future with a sense of optimism that could result in some newfound rewards.

For Reflection

🙠 Embrace the challenges in life. You may learn something.

🙠 Remember that learning is not always predictable and not always planned.

🙠 A problem may be a learning opportunity in disguise.

~47~
Read for Pleasure

Several years ago I came across a study that surveyed the amount of recreational reading done by people in 20 to 25 different professions. I fully expected to see teachers near the top of that list but was quite surprised to discover that the teaching profession was closer to the bottom of the list. I suppose my surprise was due to the fact that teachers spend a great deal of time teaching children how to read. It would be expected that we would be readers, too.

It is easy to imagine that reading student papers every night, grading quizzes, projects, and reports; drafting new lesson plans each week; and keeping up with current professional articles create an easy excuse for denying ourselves time to read for pleasure. It is sad, because as promoters of the enjoyment of reading, teachers should be models of lifelong readers. If students could observe the joy we get from reading, they too would view reading as a positive activity.

There is something even more important about regular, sustained opportunities for pleasure reading in our lives. Reading is a way to escape the stresses of our profession. By losing ourselves in a novel or some other form of pleasure reading, we can refresh and renew our thinking in magical ways. For example, I love to read murder mysteries and adventure stories. I have discovered that when I am immersed in a book, it provides a release valve for the tensions of the day. By making reading a regular part of each day, we have an opportunity to become involved in the actions, thoughts, and adventures of others. Our minds are refocused on someone else's story or tale.

Reading for pleasure is a powerful mental dynamic. I often discover that after 30 minutes of reading an engrossing book, I am able to approach a dreaded task with renewed energy and a clearer perspective. My mind has become absorbed by the imagination of the author. Making recreational reading a regular and sustained part of my week refreshes my mind and allows me to approach the duties that await me with renewed vitality. The process is simple, and the benefits are grand.

For Reflection

✦ Find a good book and read a chapter every day.

✦ Take time away from the hassles of the day and sink into a good book. Free the mind and free the soul.

✦ Teachers deal with so many facts and figures in education, it's important to turn our minds over to fictions as well.

~48~
Always Leave a Campsite Better Than You Found It

Growing up in southern California, my father and I would spend two weeks in the middle of August camping and fishing. We would pack up the car and head up Route 395 from Los Angeles toward Mammoth Lakes. We would spend the first night in a cabin, and the next day we would enlist the services of a muleskinner and several horses to take us up into the wilderness. Our destination was Jackson Lake, a nine-hour trek that took us through some of nature's most beautiful scenery.

Once we arrived at our site, we would unpack and set up camp. For days we would hike around the lake, through acres of undisturbed woods, across verdant meadows to locate some of the world's best fishing—rainbow and golden trout. It was our time together—time away from life in the big city.

It was during those fishing trips that my father taught me a very important lesson. We would fish all day, every day for almost two weeks, but on the last day, we would stay in camp to clean up, repair a wooden table, clear out part of a trail, and other such tasks. On the last day of each trip my father said, *Always leave a campsite better than you found it.* And we did. We spent the entire day fixing, cleaning, repairing, clearing out, and performing other tasks to ready the site for the next set of fishermen to visit the area.

My father's maxim has stayed with me for a long time. Leaving things better than when you found them is something I truly believe in and try to make part of my life. That conviction, I suspect, may be one of the reasons many of us became teachers. We seek to make the lives of children better.

The saying also rings true in other aspects of our lives—in our dealings with colleagues, with administrators, and with other people. When we approach people with the question, *How can I make this person's life a little better than I found it?* we are filled with a limitless sense of direction and purpose. The question requires us to give something of ourselves to make a positive change for someone else.

A simple handshake, a polite comment, a kind gesture, a thank you, or an offer of help can cause potential improvement in people's lives. Simply by waking up each day to thoughts of how we might improve the lives of those with whom we live and work, we can achieve a heightened level of personal satisfaction in our own lives.

For Reflection

❧ Be a positive influence in someone's life. The rewards are tremendous.

❧ Make it a point to improve one person's life just a little bit today. Do the same thing tomorrow.

❧ Helping others makes us kind, generous and loving.

❧ As the old song goes, *You've Got to Give a Little to Get a Little.*

~49~
Take a Mini-Vacation

Most of our lives are filled with an incredible array of tasks. It seems that here is never enough time to get things done, and all of our time is taken up with our many chores.

One simple strategy you can use to reduce of stress and to refocus on the important things is to give yourself a mini-vacation. I am not suggesting a major vacation, when you fly off to some distant tropical island and spend two weeks in a hammock. Nor do I mean a fancy resort hotel with incomparable service and a bill to match. I am suggesting a mini-vacation, an opportunity to leave responsibilities behind and enjoy some new scenery. The only stipulation is that the destination should be within an hour's drive of where you live. That allows you time to get there, quality time to spend there, and time to get home, all within a single day.

Think about your area. What places have you read about and have always wanted to experience? Has someone told you about an interesting, out of the way spot within an easy drive? Are there locations you have never taken the time to visit?

Take out a map and look for some of the following places to visit:

An arena, ballpark, ice rink
A museum, aquarium, or gallery
A mountain, swamp, or forest
A cave, beach, or valley
A theater, zoo, or library
An ocean, lake, or river
A small café or country inn
A bicycle path or hiking trail
An orchard, farm, or stable

A botanical garden or nature park
A county fair or flea market
A quarry, tide pool, or rock formation
A planetarium, winery, or hobby shop
An airport, bus, or train station
A state capitol or historical area
An ethnic restaurant or coffee shop
A home center or greenhouse
A garden center or lumberyard

Scour your local newspaper for more ideas. You may want to do what my friend Don does. He writes down each local attraction, place, or event on a separate index card and keeps them in a small file box. Each week he and his wife randomly select a card from the box. It becomes their mini-vacation for the week. These little trips provide them with unique and inexpensive opportunities to learn more about the sights and sounds around them. Most importantly, it gives them an opportunity to renew and rejuvenate themselves. They often discover things about their local area they never knew existed.

For Reflection

✣ Look around your area. There are many little getaways nearby.

✣ Leave your immediate environment to appreciate what may be just around the corner.

✣ Plan a mini-vacation every week.

✣ Explore the undiscovered and learn about the unfamiliar.

~50~
Create a Mental Image of Your Day

In her book *Simple Abundance,* Sarah Ban Breathnach likens each day to an artist's canvas. Each day we begin with a new canvas and, like every artist, we must prepare that canvas before we can add the paint. The canvas must be primed before it can be turned into a work of art. Breathnach suggests that our personal priming consist of meditation, journal writing, a slowing down to concentrate on one task at a time, and an awareness of our true preferences. These preliminary steps, she says, are necessary prerequisites for contentment.

Kathy is a second-grade teacher in a school district southwest of Denver. She has been teaching for six years, and she still has what she likes to call the *fire in the belly.* Colleagues rarely see her enter school in the morning with a sad expression on her face or with her shoulders slumped. She almost always arrives in a cheerful mood with kind words for everyone. Teachers in nearby classrooms can hear her sing as she goes about preparing her classroom for the students' morning arrival. For Kathy, each day is a positive new experience. She is one of the most cheerful teachers on staff, and her colleagues are amazed at her positive outlook toward each day.

Kathy knows that her success as a classroom teacher often depends on how well she prepares herself and how well she presents herself to her students. She knows that her attitude at the start of the day will affect the attitude of her students, so she makes a regular and conscious effort to prepare herself before she arrives at school.

When Kathy leaves for school each morning, she gives herself 15 extra minutes for the drive. She pulls into the school parking lot and turns off the car engine. Then, she sits and prepares her mind for the day ahead. Instead of just rushing into school, Kathy closes her eyes and creates a vivid mental image of the day before her. She runs this mental image through her mind, envisioning the tasks ahead, the students with whom she wants to spend extra time, the lessons she will be preparing, and the routines of the day. Kathy says this preparation time helps ensure that her day is well organized. It enables her to feel more composed which results in less stress. By taking time to visualize, Kathy prepares her mind for the events and how she will manage them.

Try it. I think you will be pleasantly surprised at how much better you will be able to maintain balance. Better still, you will experience a more positive outlook on your day and a greater feeling of control.

For Reflection

✤ Take some time each morning to create a positive image of your day.

✤ Run some mental images through your head about the events you have planned and how they will turn out.

✤ Organize your day ahead of time.

✤ See each day as a positive new adventure.

~51~
Establish One Goal

Your day is busy, and your day planner is crowded with activities. It seems as though you move from one crisis to another. By the end of the day, you wonder if you accomplished anything at all or whether your students learned anything.

If you are like most teachers, your days are filled with an overabundance of tasks, duties, and responsibilities. You may feel like that little Dutch boy who put his finger in the dike. You have stopped the water from leaking through, but there you are, stuck with your finger in the dike and not able to move. You worry that your efforts are not helping you make any progress; you seem to become so consumed by the things you need to do that you are overwhelmed.

The solution is to take a few moments at the start of the day to list one goal that you will attempt to accomplish. Focus on a single goal, rather than overwhelm yourself with a waterfall of tasks and responsibilities. Take a few minutes in the morning, before students start arriving perhaps, and write out a single goal that will be your focus for the day. The goal can be instructional, such as, *José will learn his three times table by the end of the day.* It can be a personal goal, such as, *I will not reprimand Donna once during the course of the day.* It can be collegial, *I will send the librarian a thank-you note for helping me select the literature for my social studies unit.* It might be relational, such as *I will greet the principal with a smile at the professional workshop this afternoon.* Or, it may be personal, *I will do five minutes of isometric exercises at my desk during lunch today.*

What is important is that you choose a single goal, write it down, and keep it in the forefront of your thoughts during the day. At the end of the day, take another brief period of time and review your goal. Chances are that you will have accomplished your goal. I think you will discover a great deal of satisfaction in managing your classroom experience. More importantly, you will end the school day with a sense of accomplishment. As hectic as your day may have been, you will be able to say to yourself, *I accomplished my personal goal.* What a marvelous sense of self-satisfaction!

For Reflection

❧ Establish one small personal goal each day.

❧ Work toward that goal.

❧ Evaluate your attainment of that goal at the end of the day.

❧ Record those daily attainments in a person diary or journal.

❧ Review your diary on a regular basis and note what is happening and how you feel.

~52~

The Potential to Be a Good Day

To affect the quality of the day, that is the highest of arts.
Henry David Thoreau

A few years ago I was discussing the book *Alexander and the Terrible, Horrible, No Good, Very Bad Day* by Judith Viorst with a group of third-grade students. Our conversation about Alexander was animated and stimulating. Students volunteered experiences of their own days when terrible and horrible events seemed to plague them. One student raised her hand and asked me an unforgettable question, *Do teachers ever have terrible, horrible, no good, very bad days?*

Of course they do!

I am sure that you know the kinds of events that can make some days less memorable than others do. You can recall just as many terrible and horrible examples as I can. There are events, and sometimes entire days, we would rather forget.

A friend reminded me some time ago that a day is neither good nor bad. Each day has a sunrise, and each day has a sunset. Each day is 24 hours long; each day represents one complete rotation of Earth on its axis. A day is a day is a day. They are all the same, at least from a scientific standpoint. As my friend reminded me, it is not whether a day is good or bad.

It is what we do with our day that influences our perception of it. It is our attitude that determines how good or bad the 24-hour period seems. With a positive frame of mind, we can handle whatever life throws our way.

I realize that it is the way I approach my day that determines how the day will turn out for me. Do I approach my day with spirit, determination, and love? Or, do I begin a new day dreading a parent conference, hating the lesson I have prepared for science, or detesting the faculty meeting I have to attend at the end of the school day? The choice is mine. Ultimately, the attitude and frame of mind I choose will determine the degree of joy or pleasure that I derive from my day.

For Reflection

᠅ How do you choose to approach your day?

᠅ Our perception of how a day will turn out often becomes the reality of that day.

᠅ Days aren't good or bad—we determine their success.

᠅ *Carpe Diem*—seize the day!

~53~
Your Job Is Not Your Life

Every so often I try to adjust my focus on what is truly important. Teaching is my occupation, not my life. Teaching is just one part of who I am; it is not my *raison d'être*. Please do not get me wrong—I love to teach. I love to work with young people and share with them the marvels and mysteries of the world. But as much as I love it, teaching is not the only thing in my life.

Several years ago I attended an education convention in San Diego. There were more than 15,000 teachers there from across the country and around the world. The exhibit hall at the San Diego Convention Center was filled with 500 exhibitors, publishers, educational supply houses, booksellers, and many other commercial enterprises. Teachers cruised the aisles looking for the latest materials, children's literature, teaching programs, and free posters. I, too, walked through the exhibit hall, not just to see the latest in educational publishing, but also to talk with teachers from many different schools and districts.

During my travels, I bumped into a friend I had not seen in some time. We exchanged pleasantries and brought each other up to date on our latest professional accomplishments. She had obtained her doctorate and was now working for a large school district in the Midwest as a reading supervisor. She commented on the many tasks she had taken on, how complicated her life had become, and the various opportunities her promotion provided her. Finally, I asked her, *With all those responsibilities consuming so much of your time, what do you do in your free time?* After a long pause, she sheepishly admitted that her work had become her life—she no longer had free time.

We risk falling into the habit of allowing our occupations to become the driving forces in our lives. Work seems preeminent. So much is invested in our work that there is little left for the things that we treasure. We allow our jobs to drain our energy and time, leaving little left for family, friends, and pastimes.

I encourage you to step back every so often and assess your priorities. Is your job taking over your waking hours? Is it consuming time that should be spent with family? Does it deplete the majority of your energy and spirit?

Occasional self-assessment can help you achieve balance in your life. It will not only make you a better, happier person but a better, happier teacher as well. Your job is an important part of your life, but should not interfere with living your life. Refocus. Do your job well, but also take time to live your life well.

For Reflection

❧ How much time do you devote to your work? How much do you devote to your life? Is there an imbalance?

❧ Make sure you know what is truly important in your life.

❧ Remember that no single job is ever more important than the people doing it.

❧ Is your life in balance?

~54~

Persevere

When I visit schools as an author-in-residence, I am sometimes asked which author was the most influential to me in my writing career. In response, I always share this story with my young audience:

Many years ago a young man wrote a children's story. It was his first story, and it was a major departure from the typical children's book. Nonetheless, he felt that it was a creative and dynamic way to bring literature alive for kids. He sent his manuscript out to one publishing house. A few weeks later it came back, rejected. He sent it out to another publisher, and just like the first, this one too rejected it.

Time after time he sent his manuscript out to a publisher. Time after time the manuscript came back rejected. Some of the editors commented that the book would never sell, that it was too far out of the mainstream of children's literature, or that a rhyming book just did not have a large enough market.

But the young man believed in his book. He knew it was a departure from the mainstream, but he had worked long and hard on it and knew that kids would receive it, even if adult editors were rejecting it.

After 27 rejection letters, the young man discussed the situation with a friend. His friend suggested that he send the manuscript to a particular publisher he knew, a publisher near the end of the author's alphabetical list of publishers. Once again, he sent his manuscript out, and once again, he waited. A few weeks later a letter arrived saying that a decision had been made to move ahead with its publication in spite of some reservations. The young man was elated—a publisher had finally accepted his first book, and it was finally going to be published!

The name of the book was *And to Think That I Saw It on Mulberry Street*. The author was Theodore Geisel, known as Dr. Suess.

I keep a framed copy of that book above my computer. Whenever I receive a rejection letter from a publisher or receive a negative comment from a colleague, I glance at that book and remember that Ted Geisel once received 27 rejection letters for a project he truly believed in. Dr. Suess persevered, and because of his perseverance and belief in his work, the world of children's literature was changed forever. Believe in something and stand up for it—the world will be a better place.

For Reflection

❧ Hold fast to what you believe in.

❧ Establish goals and don't let go.

❧ Some form of rejection always precedes acceptance.

~55~

The "Who" in Your Teaching

The pressures of cramming so much curriculum material into too little time causes us to lose focus on the children. I have experienced this several times in my teaching career. I am bogged down with standards, expectations, goals, and objectives, and a hundred other *must-do's* in my instructional day. I find myself getting so wrapped up in teaching all the requirements, that I lose sight of the fact that I should be teaching people. It is an occupational hazard—the *what* of teaching begins to supercede the *who*.

Recently, I was invited into a classroom as a visiting author. The students had been well prepared for my visit and bombarded me with insightful questions. I shared a slide program with them that illustrated where I get the ideas for my children's books and how I develop those ideas. It was a fast-paced hour, and the students were engaged throughout.

As is my custom, I like to chat with teachers during a visit. I especially like to tap into their storehouses of information on how I can become a better teacher. So, I asked one teacher, *If given the opportunity, what one piece of advice would you offer every teacher in the country?* She thought for a moment, and then shared this with me.

Put the kids first. Make a difference in their lives. No one ever went to the grave wishing they had achieved higher standardized test scores.

I have seldom heard a better teaching philosophy.

For Reflection

❧ Take time to see the individuals in your classroom as human beings, rather than simply as students.

❧ Do you truly know the people behind the names?

❧ Are you spending more time teaching children or more time teaching reading, math, writing, spelling, social studies, and science?

~56~

Achieve a Sense of Balance

A friend of mine has an amazing outlook on life. Always happy, always content, she is the epitome of a self-actualized woman. She has a kind word for everyone she works with, and she consistently models joy and energy with her students throughout the school year. She is, in many ways, a model teacher and a model individual.

In conversation one day, she shared with me an important lesson that she learned many years ago. Like most teachers, she has plenty of stress in her life, and she is willing to accept that. But, it was what she told me about how she handles that stress that made the most sense. She says that her definition of stress management is not just what she does for herself (internal), but also what she does for others (external).

She informed me that achieving a balance between her internal and external objectives is what helps her stay on an even keel. She devotes a certain amount of time to herself, and she spends an equal amount of time on others. For example, she rewards herself with an occasional note about an important task she completed and how well she did it. In addition, she takes a few minutes to write a colleague a complimentary note about all the planning that went into the school's science fair. She takes time from her busy schedule to indulge herself in a massage at the local health club. At the same time, she makes a point to hug each of her students when they arrive in the morning.

For her, stress management is balance. She knows that she will never eliminate the stress in her life, but she believes that she can better manage stress because she takes care of herself and takes care of the important people in her life, too. Her stress management plan is a win-win situation.

Achieving balance is not easy; it takes work. However, when we give to others *and* give to ourselves, we can make a difference in our lives and in the lives of those around us.

For Reflection

✤ Make sure that you plan to give to someone else, as well as to yourself, each day.

✤ Pamper yourself as much as you pamper others.

✤ Remember that stress has both internal and external sources. We need to find internal and external ways to balance stress

~57~
Actively Seek Happiness

Do you pursue happiness or do you wait for happiness to come into your life? A friend once confided to me, *Happiness is not something that happens, it's something that is pursued.* I, too, think that happiness is an active, rather than a passive, state.

It is sad to think that there are people who wait around for happiness to tap them on the shoulder and enter their lives. They believe that if they just wait long enough, happiness will find them, and life will be forever changed. Too often, they keep waiting and waiting and. . .

If you ask the average person what happiness is, he or she might tell you that it is a state of mind—a state of joy or euphoria that brightens the spirit and enriches the soul. In a sense that is correct, but true happiness is a work in progress. Happiness does not simply occur; rather, it is created through an active commitment to its attainment.

Happiness is achieved by setting goals, establishing priorities, and organizing your life. The active pursuit of happiness is an active commitment to doing those things that ensure its generation. I am suggesting that happiness in life will be realized when we are determined to achieve it.

The real truth of life is that happiness is attainable. When we establish goals and directions for our life, happiness becomes a natural and normal by-product. When we sit and wait for life to happen, happiness eludes us. Happiness requires activity, not passivity.

Think about the things that make you happy—a child's laugh, a warm summer's day, or an action-packed novel. In each case, someone had to do work in order for that happiness to occur. Someone told a joke and caused a child to laugh. Someone took a walk outside and reaped the reward of a beautiful summer day. Someone wrote a book to bring happiness to the reader. In each case, happiness was the reward of activity. Happiness was produced, not just a chance occurrence.

So it is with our lives. When we actively seek happiness, happiness results. On the other hand, if we wait for happiness to occur, it may never happen. Remember that happiness is an active term. Look for it, create it, nurture it, and enjoy it.

For Reflection

❧ Engage in activity to set the stage for happiness.

❧ Keep in mind that happiness is an active verb.

❧ Happiness comes about through the attainment of personal goals.

❧ Remember when you first learned to ride a bike? You were happy because you had attained a self-established goal.

~58~
Take Ten Minutes

To affect the quality of the day, that is the highest of arts.
Henry David Thoreau

It is one of those days. Three parents are coming in for conferences. You are expected to attend a meeting to choose a new science textbook series. The principal asks you to join another committee. A child gets sick on someone else's jacket. Two students have dental appointments and need assignments. The reading lesson bombs. The class guinea pig escapes. Someone hits her head on a cabinet door. The secretary wants you to stop by the office during lunch. You know it is going to be a long, long day.

Teachers do many things for many people every day. Our students need our attention, the administrators require record keeping and more, parents request time to speak with us, and our colleagues need our input on committees and help with school functions. It seems as though we are doing so many things for so many people that we seldom have time for ourselves. At the end of the day we drag ourselves home only to realize that we have a stack of papers to grade or lesson plans to write. We are exhausted and know that tomorrow we will have to do it all over again.

Years ago, during a conversation at a social gathering, I was describing all the time and task demands placed on teachers.

I used the analogy of a mouse on the wheel in its cage. I said that teachers often feel like that mouse—the faster they run, the more they stay in one place.

I began to plan ten minutes of *down time* into every day. It may be ten minutes during lunchtime. It might be ten minutes after everyone has left for the day, but it is *my* ten minutes. I may use that time to read part of an adventure novel or take a short nap. I may want to use the time to write a letter to a friend or a section of a new book. I may use the time to think about my wife and children, or I may choose to do nothing at all.

I have realized, as have many of my colleagues, that ten minutes can refresh my mind, help me sort out what is important, and allow me clearer perspective. Nothing will eliminate the tasks and responsibilities of my day, but a short break helps me cleanse my mind and slow down the action around me. This mental break provides me with sufficient refreshment to tackle the rest of the day with renewed energy and commitment. Most importantly, it gives me an anchor point for the day. Interestingly, I have discovered that these short breaks have reduced my end of the day fatigue. I have given something as valuable to myself as I try to give to those around me every day.

For Reflection

&⅋⅌ Give yourself a mental break every day.

&⅋⅌ Everybody needs a vacation. Make one a regular part of your daily activities.

&⅋⅌ Disengage your mind from the feverish pace of the day—ten minutes is all you may need.

~59~
The Story of Your Life

In her book *Take Time for Your Life*, personal coach Cheryl Richardson suggests that readers should use a daily journal. She says that "captur[ing] the story of your life . . . is a powerful exercise in honoring who you are and where you've come from."

Richardson suggests that we separate our lives into decades and then respond to a series of open-ended statements. Some of these statements include:

The significant events during this part of my life were . . .
The person(s) who influenced me most was (were) . . .
This part of my life affects me now in the following way . . .

She says that our responses will help reveal personality traits that may be hindering our personal advancement. They may also indicate patterns that get in the way of personal fulfillment and satisfaction.

I could not agree with her more. As philosopher George Santayana once said, *Those who cannot remember the past are condemned to repeat it.* What we are today has been shaped in large measure by the events and circumstances of our personal history. How we recall or reflect on those past events, our perceptions, are often more important than the actual events themselves.

An interesting variation of Richardson's exercise is to separate your teaching career into five-year blocks of time. (Newer teachers should separate their careers into one-year blocks of time.) Record each block of time in a journal, and then, for each block, respond to each of the following open-ended statements:

- The most influential person was . . .
- The most memorable event was . . .
- The greatest change I made was . . .
- The most meaningful thing I learned was . . .
- The greatest thrill I had was . . .
- The most important thing I learned was . . .

Complete the recording of your thoughts and take a careful look at your responses. Did the majority of your responses center on school-related items or did the majority of the responses focus on personal items? Did you tend to emphasize one aspect of your life more than another, or is there some sense of harmony and balance in your responses?

What you will discover is a greater appreciation of yourself and a greater appreciation for your ability to change and grow. You will be able to see progress in your comments. You may also be able to identify areas that need strengthening or a little more work in the coming year(s). Most importantly, having taken a look at yourself from the inside out, you will deepen your self-understanding.

For Reflection

❧ Knowing where you have been will help you with where you want to go.

❧ Take time to think about the significant events of your life and how they have helped shape the person you are today. What importance will you give to the events of today that will help to shape the person you will become tomorrow?

❧ How will today be better than yesterday? What will you do to make it so?

~60~

Time Out for You

One of my favorite "Far Side" cartoons by Gary Larson shows a group of students in a classroom. One student is raising his hand and asks, *Mr. Osborne, may I be excused? My brain is full.* I like this cartoon for several reasons, including the fact that it reveals a universal truth about teaching and teachers. Although Larson frequently gives education and teachers a gentle jab, he points out that education is a part of everyday life.

No doubt, there have been times in your teaching career when you have reached your saturation point—the point in your day when you have given everything , and you have no more left to give. You realize that you are near the end of your emotional or professional *rope.* Your brain is full.

Meanwhile, there are other things to do. There is a social studies lesson to teach, field trip permission slips to collect, a poster to place in the hallway, and a thousand other things to accomplish. But, your brain is full! If you are like most teachers, you just keep plowing ahead. There is a schedule to adhere to, standards to teach, and a limited amount of time available for the thousand things left on the *To Do* list.

Time out! Plowing ahead when we are physically, emotionally, and intellectually drained is self-defeating and self-destructive. Forcing ourselves to move on when we are drained results in a half-hearted job. Under these circumstances, little teaching takes place and much too little learning.

One of the most useful teaching strategies you can implement is a *time out* strategy. Let students know that you have reached the point of overload. You may be tired or mentally drained because of particular events or circumstances. That is all right; it is perfectly human, and I believe it is perfectly human to let students know how you feel. Tell them, *I am really feeling overwhelmed now, let us take a 15-minute "brain break" and read something at our desks.* This simple decision can create a marvelous learning opportunity. It signals to students that learning does not have to be non-stop from 9:00 in the morning to 3:30 in the afternoon. It suggests that the learning process is not a straight path from A to B. Learning is continuous, but not necessarily sequential.

Students need to know that you are human. You do not always have to be *on* to be effective. You need mental breaks and so do your students. If needed, take some time during regular classroom activities to *chill out*, regroup, and revitalize. Refresh your mind and your thinking about the tasks before you. A needed 15-minute break can do wonders for your teaching effectiveness and for your students' appreciation of you as a human being.

For Reflection

❧ Don't be afraid to let students see your human side. After all, we are models for the individuals we want our students to become.

❧ Provide sufficient opportunities for others to see you as you really are.

❧ Everybody needs an occasional time out. Do not deny yourself time to regenerate or reinvigorate your mind and soul.

~61~

A Do-It-Yourself Project

Every year I resolve to be a little less the *me I know*
and leave a little room for the *me I could be.*
Wendy Wasserstein

Several years ago I had the pleasure of collaborating with a colleague on a series of professional workshops. She and I had been contracted to do several seminars in selected school districts in the South. The workshops focused on practices that would help teachers develop more dynamic classroom curricula, using some of the latest and most effective grouping strategies.

My friend has a distinctive and positive outlook on the teaching profession and on life. She says, *Life is a do-it-your-self project.* It is her belief that the best and most successful classrooms are places in which teachers continuously learn and grow with their students. She believes that the ideas we share with teachers during workshops are just ideas—they only achieve potency when teachers implement them. As teachers grow, so will ideas.

Teachers help students grow and change. We spend considerable time adding to their knowledge base and skills and to their affective development. We believe that our students have the capacity to grow and change, and we devote our time and effort to helping that become a reality.

We do ourselves a great disservice when we fail to take the time to realize our own capacity for growth. Too often, we think that because we have a college degree or that we have been teaching for x number of years, we have our acts together. We know the procedures, the rules, and the expectations of classroom and school life. We know what we have to do, and we get it done. But, we find ourselves in a mental rut because we have standardized our lives as much as we have standardized the curriculum.

When we acknowledge the potential for growth in our lives, we celebrate the possibilities for self-improvement and self-development. People who resist change and say, *That's the way we've always done it* dismay me. The implication is that if it worked in the past, it will surely work in the future. Coping with the world by clinging to the past makes life static, stagnant, and unrewarding.

Teachers, like doctors, plumbers, auto mechanics, and others with a job to do, are imperfect people living and working in a changing world. The value of embracing change is to realize our capacity for growth and development. Growing, changing, and becoming do not end with adolescence, college, or adulthood—they are lifelong journey that should be celebrated.

For Reflection

⁂ Acknowledge the capacity for continued growth in your own life.

⁂ Accept your limitations and use them as springboards for greater learning opportunities.

⁂ Change is inevitable. It is a normal part of the growth process. Recognize your potential for change and for growth.

~62~
A Few Thoughts

Here are several ideas to think about. Choose one, write it on a piece of paper, and put it on your desk tomorrow morning. Then, do it!

- Work like you don't need the money.

- Love like you've never been hurt.

- Sing even if you can't carry a tune.

- Dance like you do when nobody's watching.

- Wonder like a child.

- Hold hands with yourself.

- Hug someone new.

- Appreciate yesterday, love today, and anticipate tomorrow.

- Ask questions without answers.

- Imagine the improbable; dream the impossible.

- Love yourself—you're the best you have.

❧ Laugh like there's no tomorrow; then do it again the next day.

❧ Make love, not war (I'm a child of the 60s!).

❧ Practice patience with yourself.

❧ Begin every day with love; end it the same way, too.

❧ You're a princess or prince—grant someone's wish!

Reflect ~ My Thoughts

Refocus ~ My Goals

Recharge ~ My Actions

What are you already happy with in your professional life?

Where do you see opportunities for change or improvement?

Who might be able to support you?

What will you need in order to achieve this goal?

How will you communicate your needs to others?

What is one simple change you can make to get started?

Resources

I am often asked for suggestions of self-help books that will provide colleagues with information on how they can become better teachers and better human beings. Suffice it to say that there is a plethora of resources of every size, philosophy, and persuasion on the marketplace.

As I reviewed the material in this book and sought to find authors who were in agreement with these ideas, I kept coming back to the same five books. These books, although not written specifically for teachers, provide valuable and immediately useful ideas for all of us. The authors are direct, forward, and uncompromising in their suggestions. Their philosophies, and mine, are based on a single universal truth: *We cannot take care of others until we first take care of ourselves.*

My advice—obtain all of these books! Although I've tried to arrange the titles in priority order, admittedly, this list reflects my own conscious biases. Borrow these books from friends, check them out of your local library, or purchase them. Read one in concert with this book. I sincerely believe you will discover myriad possibilities for a more satisfying and enjoyable life. I know you will become a better human being, and I am equally convinced you will become a better teacher.

Don't Sweat the Small Stuff . . . and It's All Small Stuff by Richard Carlson (New York: Hyperion, 1997). If you can buy only one book, make it this one. This book started it all and remains one of the best. It is straightforward and provides simple advice that can be used by anyone. The hundred essays are easy to digest, and the ideas are easy to implement. It is a book to revisit time and time again. It should have a permanent place on every teacher's desk.

Simple Abundance: A Daybook of Comfort and Joy by Sarah Ban Breathnach (New York: Warner Books, 1995). This is one of the most engaging and practical self-help books I have ever read. The author's reflections and ruminations give every person, female or male, much to think about. Ms. Breathnach puts a premium on time for us and time for our own self-renewal, a process, she affirms, that must be done systematically and on a regular basis. This is another book to keep in one's professional library.

Take Time for Your Life by Cheryl Richardson (New York: Broadway Books, 1999). The author, a personal coach, provides readers with a seven-step plan for reinvigorating their lives and getting more out of life. The reading is easy, but some of the suggestions will take energy and commitment. The results are worth it because, as the author avows, we grow best when we grow from within. The book is filled with many resources and practical ideas for everyone.

Life Strategies: Doing What Works, Doing What Matters by Phillip McGraw (New York: Hyperion, 1999). If you're looking for a no-nonsense approach to self-renewal and self-improvement, this is the book. The author hits you right between the eyes. He pulls no punches and never sugarcoats his advice. One of the most practical books I've read, the author hits every mark with a direct and forward style that doesn't mince words or dance around the issues. This book will definitely get you thinking and, most importantly, doing!

Stress Management for Dummies by Allen Elkin (Foster City, CA: IDG Books, 1999). I know that you are not wondering why I included this book on the list. This volume overflows with down-to-earth practical advice that any person, in or out of education, can use. Here, you'll discover a wealth of easy-to-use ideas, strategies and techniques that can seriously reduce the stress in your life and bring more harmony into your career.

Personal Journal Pages

RIGBY BEST TEACHERS PRESS

Personal Journal Pages

Personal Journal Pages

RIGBY BEST TEACHERS PRESS

Personal Journal Pages

About the Author

Tony Fredericks is a nationally recognized expert in elementary science and reading education. He is well known for his energetic, fast-paced, and informative presentations. His dynamic assemblies have captivated thousands of children and teachers from coast to coast and border to border—all with rave reviews. Tony's background includes more than three decades as a classroom teacher, curriculum coordinator, reading specialist, staff developer, author, professional storyteller, and renowned expert in children's literature.

With more than 55 teacher resource books to his credit, Tony is also the author of more than two dozen highly acclaimed children's books. Celebrated children's titles include *Under One Rock: Bugs, Slugs and Other Ughs* (Dawn Publications), *Zebras* (Lerner), *Cannibal Animals: Animals That Eat Their Own Kind* (Watts), *Elephants for Kids* (NorthWord), *In One Tidepool: Crabs, Snails and Salty Tails* (Dawn Publications) and *Tsunami Man: Learning About Killer Waves with Walter Dudley* (University of Hawaii Press). He visits many schools throughout the United States each year.

Tony is currently a professor of education at York College in York, Pennsylvania. There, he teaches elementary methods courses in reading, language arts, and science. Additionally he maintains a children's author website specifically designed for classrooms and schools around the country (www.AFredericks.com).